# TEAK-WALLAH

REGINALD CAMPBELL.

# TEAK-WALLAH

## THE ADVENTURES OF
## A YOUNG ENGLISHMAN IN THAILAND
## IN THE 1920s

*By*
REGINALD CAMPBELL

*ILLUSTRATED*

SINGAPORE OXFORD NEW YORK
OXFORD UNIVERSITY PRESS
1986

*Oxford University Press*
*Oxford New York Toronto*
*Petaling Jaya Singapore Hong Kong Tokyo*
*Delhi Bombay Calcutta Madras Karachi*
*Nairobi Dar es Salaam Cape Town*
*Melbourne Auckland*
*and associates in*
*Beirut Berlin Ibadan Nicosia*
*OXFORD is a trade mark of Oxford University Press*

*ISBN 0 19 582648 5*

*Printed in Malaysia by Peter Chong Printers Sdn. Bhd.*
*Published by Oxford University Press Pte. Ltd.*
*Unit 221, Ubi Avenue 4, Singapore 1440*

# To PAN

## AUTHOR'S NOTE

My warm thanks are due to Mr. W. A. Elder, who kindly supplied twelve out of the fifteen photographs in this book.

# CONTENTS

# CONTENTS

# LIST OF ILLUSTRATIONS

# CHAPTER ONE

## THE JOURNEY OUT

I HAD said good-bye to my naval friends, and was running away from sea to the land: a reversal of the usual prelude to adventure, I reflected, as the train bore me rapidly south from Edinburgh; but for me ships and seas and the whining roll of a man-of-war held nothing of romance, however much they might appeal to others. *I* loved the land, with *its* ever-changing moods; for me land promised adventure, and I looked like getting it, bound as I was for the far-distant teak forests of Northern Siam.

A forest assistant in the teak jungles: that was what I, an ex-naval officer, had somewhat startlingly become, and I tried to picture what the job would be like. I pictured myself tramping between steaming walls of green, a solar topee on my head, sweat upon my brow, and a long line of carrier coolies behind me; I pictured another teak man, with his retinue, suddenly appearing round a bend, and I saw myself greeting him as Stanley greeted Livingstone. Curiously enough, these innocent expectations came remarkably close to the real thing, I was to discover.

I arrived in London, swirling and chaotic in the aftermath of war. I repaired to an outfitter's, and bought an enormous quantity of entirely useless kit at an enormous price (specially thin pyjamas, for instance, which I never wore the whole five years I was in Siam, black Chinese trousers and cotton singlets taking their place). I then went to the Head Office of the teak firm that had engaged me. They said:

" You're entitled under your agreement to a first-class passage, but what with the shortage of ships and the numbers of men wanting to get out East we don't know how to find you one. Wonder if you'd mind going by the s.s. *Blank*? She's advertised as first-class for food, but only third for accommodation, so of course we can't compel you . . ."

I interrupted by giving what I hoped was not too scornful a laugh. Third-class accommodation in a merchant vessel? What cared I for that after seven years of hammock and sea-chest—with occasional cabin—in ships of the Royal Navy? It would be a luxury, a luxury made all the more enjoyable now that the war was over and a torpedo wasn't likely at any moment to precipitate one into the nether depths.

And so, on a brave May morning, did I sail in the s.s. *Blank* from Liverpool for the Far East. She was, I found, an ordinary cargo-carrying vessel of about 7,000 tons converted by means of specially built superstructure into a cargo-cum-passenger craft. There were 150 of us passengers, all males—women were not allowed to be carried, for reasons that I was quick to discover—and a glance round told me that the accommodation was of the crudest; we fed in two herds in a far too small saloon, our tiny cabins were four-bunked and entirely devoid of ventilation, the deck space for exercise was almost nil, and the bath and lavatory arrangements were past praying for.

The passengers themselves were about the most mixed lot imaginable, and reminded me of a George Morrow drawing picturing all the various kinds of animals humped together in the Ark. There were two naval commanders, one of whom was so disgusted with his surroundings that he sulked in his cabin, like Achilles in his tent, for the whole of the voyage; there were gigantic ex-Lifeguardsmen; there were hard-bitten old skippers of China coasting vessels, alcoholic mates and engineers of ditto, public works men, new chums, old stiffs, commercials, men of every conceivable profession and appearance.

There were no electric fans anywhere for us passengers, and by the time we had entered the Mediterranean the situation was further improved by the ship running out of all drinks save gin, and all fresh water except for drinking purposes. Washing had to be done in salt water, as a result of which I gave up shaving and developed a hirsute growth that frightened even myself.

By the time we entered the Red Sea the few stewards there were more or less chucked their hands in, as well they might: for the general conditions in which they had to work were simply appalling. We, the passengers, took to sleeping on the iron deck, carrying our own bedding up, and you lay, with your face on someone's feet and your feet on someone's face, listening to a chorus of groans and snorts till oblivion came. In the morning you removed your face from the feet and vice versa, brushed off the collection of " stokers " or smuts which lay all over you from the funnels, and staggered down below with the bedding. In an atmosphere that would have made Satan envious you then removed, with the aid of some warm, sticky salt water, a little of the worst of the grime from face and ears and neck, then repaired to the saloon for breakfast. A real wash? One went without. And one survived.

When we entered the Indian Ocean conditions became even worse, for the monsoon was on, and with seas continually sweeping the decks accommodation was more limited than ever. Whether we wanted to or not we all had to sleep below, and by day the demand for gin, still the only drink on board, became somewhat heavy.

The "bar" consisted of an upright sort of kennel just big enough for the sweaty, pock-marked barman and his gin bottles. In order to get a drink you had to queue up, glass in hand, and gradually shuffle forward till your turn came, after which, the precious drink clutched in your hand, you would edge your way back to the crowded saloon tables and join in a game of cards or have a yarn with some particular crony.

What with the drink and the general overcrowding and complete lack of any privacy, it wasn't long before scraps began to develop, and soon it was quite a common thing to hear a shuffling and panting and swiping going on outside the saloon or down the cabin corridors.

This atmosphere of fighting became extraordinarily infectious, and on one occasion, I remember, I fell foul of one of my cabin-mates, a short, thick-set commercial travelling for a famous perfumery firm. The quarrel, as usual, was about the merest nothing, and we squared up on the reeling deck of the cabin, bristling like dogs and growling in our throats. Quite a crowd gathered in the passage, expecting to see some fun, but they were disappointed; we suddenly, perhaps because we were in reality scared stiff of one another, shook hands and, pushing through the mob, joined the rear of the inevitable queue forming up for the pock-faced barman.

We came to Colombo, and here, for the first occasion since leaving Liverpool, the ship stayed long enough for passengers to go ashore. Now, while serving my seven years in the Navy, I had spent four in the Near East; I knew Turkey—Constantinople, Gallipoli, Smyrna—the Syrian coast, Port Said, the Grecian Archipelago and so on, pretty well; but it *was* the Near East, a part that to me consisted mostly of dagoes and smells, and I had always longed for the Far, which consisted—or so I had imagined—of natives and scents. Colombo was for me the stepping-off place for the latter, and so, after lowering the Plimsoll line of my washing an inch or two, I made all haste to get ashore.

I wasn't disappointed in Colombo, indeed I revelled in the place. The trees, the flowers, the scents (yes, real scents instead of smells), seemed like Paradise after the crowded, stuffy ship, but I was brought back abruptly to realities that night.

All passengers had to be on board by 10 p.m., and in the main they obeyed the rule in so far as getting to the bottom of the gangway; the trouble then was that a good many were quite incapable of reaching the top.

Those of us already aboard got swiftly to work. Head of us was an old-timer who had done his whack out East before the war and who, having come back to join up, was on his way out again. In common with several others of his kidney, he was much revered by us new chums; he wore, for example, a " sarong " round his waist on every possible occasion, a garment at which we gazed in awe and envy; he would spout Malay words whenever possible, and was wont to hint darkly at various bouts of blackwater fever. As for malaria, he was apparently so used to it that he regarded it almost as a pet. Now, certainly, he proved a tower of strength, for he got us speedily organised carrying drunk after drunk up the ladder and down below, where we heaved them on the deck outside the saloon.

A big man himself, he did two men's work, and all the time he kept singing a refrain that went:

> " Off to old Shienghai,
>      My boys,
> Off to old Shienghai."

I suppose there were other words, but I never heard them, and soon I was singing " Off to old Shienghai," as I handled the tights up the gangway, and feeling the very devil of a fellow. Those hard-bitten old sailing-ship skippers had nothing on me!

We sailed and, tired, I turned in. The last drunk I saw was squatting outside the saloon, hands down on the deck by his sides like an ape, glassy of eye, and every now and then emitting a sort of gurgling groan that made most unpleasant hearing. He was a decent, quiet type normally, and it was rather surprising to see him thus. But nobody took any

THE AUTHOR WITH SCLAVE IN NAKON.

particular notice of him, and it was lucky he didn't die in the night.

Between Colombo and Singapore I was aware of a further subtle change in the air. It was warmer, damper, more tropical still, as though the deserts of Arabia had lost the last vestiges of influence on the climate and the jungle-fringed East at last had its own free sway and will.

On board, the drinking became heavier still; it was as though the Colombo excesses had whetted the appetites of the soaks amongst us. One fellow, the mate of some China coasting vessel, I gathered, now lived in a perpetual state of soddenness; he wasn't noisy, or offensive in any way; he just sprawled about, a sodden lump of flesh pickled in alcohol; if a limb of his happened to be in your way as you passed, you just picked it up and threw it aside, where it stayed put. I often wonder what happened to him.

By the time we reached Singapore, where I was due to disembark, seven of our passengers were down with alcoholic poisoning and under the care of the young doctor. And yet, when I came to leave the ship, with all its filth and brawling, I did so with no nasty taste in the mouth. Nor, right up to this time of writing fifteen years later, can I ever think of her with repugnance.

For, paradoxically, she was a happy ship. And she was happy because the passengers, motley lot though they were, were a loyal crowd. In spite of the numerous scraps, there was no bullying the weaker man, and when anyone got into real trouble all were ready at once to help him. There was the " goop," for instance, a regular " mummy's darling,"

B

bound for Borneo and on his first trip out from home: he lost all his money, including the cash provided him by his firm for getting on from Singapore to Borneo, in gambling at *vingt-et-un*, and when his state became known we passed the hat round and raised almost as much as he'd parted with. Then there was the " dope-doctor," an old-timer, but a wreck of a man if ever I saw one; his eyes held that glitter peculiar to dopists, yet there wasn't a soul on board who wouldn't give up a decent place on deck or in the saloon for him; because *he* was a kind, generous-hearted fellow, and we were sorry for his ghastly failing.

In Singapore I stayed three days at Raffles Hotel while waiting for the little weekly steamer that plied up the Gulf of Siam, and on my first night in the hotel I fell into a trap that must have puzzled a good many new-comers to the East. After five weeks of filth a bath was indicated, and it was in an ecstatic frame of mind that I repaired to the bathroom. Here to my dismay was no gleaming white bath with hot and cold taps; instead, I was staring at a huge jar which reminded me of Ali Baba and the Forty Thieves. But with this difference: the thieves' jars had been big enough to hide a man, but mine certainly wasn't. It was invitingly full of clean, fresh water, but though I tried first one leg and then the other, nothing could get me right in and I had to be content with feebly splashing my face with my hands. It seemed written that I wasn't to have that bath!

It wasn't till next day that I discovered a large pannikin behind the jar, and that it was the custom to dash the water over one's body with it, the water being allowed to go freely over the floor before running away through a drain in the side.

I celebrated my departure from Singapore by leaving all my luggage behind in Raffles Hotel through a misunderstanding with the runner; consequently I joined the little s.s. *Kuala* with only the clothes I stood up in. The three-day voyage up the Gulf passed very pleasantly in spite of my lack of a change, and the ship arrived at the mouth of Siam's great river Mae Nam just as dusk was falling on a rainy night. Here, before going up the twelve miles of river that still separated us from Bangkok, we had to await the tide to take us across the bar (a tiny white child was on board, and the skipper of the *Kuala* was resolved to reach the city that night in order to save her from the attentions of the mosquitoes already swarming in from the shore), and while we were at anchor I stood and gazed around me.

I was at the gateway of Siam, the great unknown into which I was to penetrate five hundred miles to take up my strange new career. Up into the darkness ribboned the broad, yellow river, with flat mangrove swamps on either side of it; Chinese coolies, fanning themselves with one hand and working with the other, so terrible were the mosquitoes at the point, toiled in cumbrous, barge-like junks close by; bull-frogs roared harshly from the swamps, and fireflies danced in thousands. Presently we moved ahead through a roar of rain up the river, and soon we had arrived at Siam's capital, the so-called Venice of the East, where we tied up alongside a wharf.

Contrary to expectations, no one from my firm

was there to meet me. (I discovered afterwards
that a telegram of mine from Singapore had mis-
carried.) Thus I found myself, minus my kit, which
was now on its way up by a later boat from Singapore, utterly alone on the wharf of a strange town,
in pitch darkness and rain that was stupendous.
Eventually a passing European, to whom I explained
my plight, hailed a gharry for me and told the Indian
driver in the Siamese language to take me to the
mess of my firm. I got in the gharry and the tiny
ponies were whipped into a trot.

We drove for miles through flare-lit streets crowded
with Siamese and Chinese and pigs and ducks and
gharries and rickshaws, then, turning off along a
quiet lane, came to a stop opposite an imposing-
looking house. I got out and looked for the bell.
There was no bell, apparently. I shouted, to receive
no answer, the house merely gaping at me blankly
through a shroud of rain. I walked up and down
the lane, but could see no signs of life anywhere.
Recollecting that someone in the *Kuala* had mentioned
the Oriental Hotel as one in which Europeans could
stay, I returned to the driver:

" Go to the Oriental Hotel," I yelled to him as
loudly as I could.

" Huh." He picked up the reins and I jumped
in the gharry again. The ponies trotted back up the
lane, then down the flare-lit road the way we had
come. Good! The Englishman's method of shrieking his own language at the top of his voice had, as
usual, penetrated the thick skull of the native and
made him understand what was required. I felt
rather proud of myself.

I was speedily disillusioned; for of a sudden the driver pulled his ponies to a halt and called to a khaki-clad gentleman who was evidently a gendarme.

" Oriental Hotel. I want to go to the Oriental Hotel," I bawled to the gendarme.

He looked blank, and a crowd collected. " Hotel. Oriental Hotel," I howled again and again.

" Hoten," said somebody brightly at last. " Hoten, Hoten."

" Ah—Hoten ! " The driver, the gendarme, everyone in the crowd suddenly understood. Smiles and bows were exchanged, the ponies were whipped up once more, and eventually I was thankfully registering my name in the longed-for Oriental.

As I crept through my mosquito net that night a foot-long " towkay " lizard regarded me balefully from the wall, and the last thing I heard was his queer cry penetrating the insect-singing darkness of the room. And so to sleep, to dream of twenty-foot dragons chasing me through the saloon of the s.s. *Blank*.

## CHAPTER TWO

## I GO UP-COUNTRY

I STOOD before the General Manager of my firm in his Bangkok office. The *contretemps* of the previous night had been explained, and there remained only a few details to settle before my going up north.

"You'll live on the country when you're up there," he informed me. "Chickens and so on from the villages. But stores like flour and sugar and tea you'll have to get down here. Buan Suan Hli's as good as anyone. The Chinese grocer in the New Road. . . . You a teetotaller, by the way?"

I replied in the negative.

"Better include a case of whisky in your order, then. A nip at night 'll keep the malaria away." The manager paused, and shot out a hand. "Goodbye," said he. "Good luck. I think you'll like the life."

I left him to his papers in the damp heat of the office, and repaired to the Chinese grocer, Buan Suan Hli. Here, after the food restrictions of the War, I wallowed in an orgy of buying. There seemed no limit to the resources of the almond-eyed gentleman who served me. Sugar? Yes, best Hong-Kong. How much did Mister want? Six tins? Right! Down went six tins on a list that rapidly assumed enormous proportions.

There followed a visit to Whiteaway Laidlaw's, where I bought my camp kit: camp bed, chair, table, mosquito net, bottle filters, crockery and plate, and then, after a night spent in the mess, I caught the early morning train for the north.

All that day the train passed through dull, flat land: first paddy-land, then mere tufted swamp devoid of any interest. After twelve hours of monotonous progress we pulled into the town of Pitsanuloke, and I walked over to the railway rest-house. There, also staying the night but travelling in the opposite direction, was a very fat little Italian couple with a most amusing baby.

We fed in the stuffy dining-room, waited on by a quiet Chinese boy, with lizards scuttling on the walls and the rain pounding down on the roof.

" What ees zis? " queried the Italian, balancing a leather-like object—the course after the soup—on his fork.

" It's fish," I replied dubiously, " when you get through the skin."

He gaped at me. " Ah, I like a jolly fellow," he cried suddenly. " You make-a da fun, eh? " And he laughed at my innocent remark till his whole little body shook. And the fat little wife laughed. And the fat baby in the adjoining room woke up and laughed too. Whereat, though I was tired and hot and hungry, it occurred to me that Siam wasn't such a bad place after all.

I went to bed, carefully placing my shoes outside the door for cleaning. I was up early next day to catch the train, and when I shouted to the Chinese boy for my shoes he merely looked blank. I summoned the fat Italian, who could speak Siamese, and explained the situation. He appeared serious, comically so.

" Why did you leave your shoes outside ze bedroom door? " he demanded.

" To be cleaned, of course," I replied.

" Eh? "

" To be cleaned," I repeated.

" I do not understand," he said gravely, shaking his head.

" In England we leave our shoes outside our doors at night if we want them cleaned," was all I was able to explain.

" Ees zat so? " said he. " Well. In Siam you leave zem outside eef you want zem stolen. Plenty t'ief here, see? "

I saw. I paid my reckoning, said good-bye to the little Italian and his fat wife and baby, and walked in my slippers over to the train. I was learning.

Not long after leaving Pitsanuloke the train entered a completely different type of country, and soon the railway track was winding up and down rolling hills clad in thick, dark green jungle. At times the track went over deep ravines, and I had glimpses of foaming, amber-coloured rivers swirling round rocks far below.

My heart beat quicker, for here were the surroundings in which I was to live for years on end. I gazed eagerly out of the window, trying to make out which were teak trees out of the numerous forest trees on either side of the track, but all that met my eyes was a vast mass of vegetation, part trees, part creeper, part grass and bushes, bound together in one indescribable whole and shrouded in grey monsoon rain.

Occasionally we stopped at tiny stations, mere strips of earth cleared from the jungle and with tiny attap-roofed, palm-fringed hamlets behind them. The villagers waiting on these stations were quite different from the Siamese and Chinese in Bangkok; they were, in fact, the Laos who inhabit the northern part of Siam, and I was favourably impressed; the men looked workmanlike in their dark blue pants of jungle cloth, and the women neat and pretty with their long, coiled-up dark hair and many-coloured "sinns," or petticoats.

Thirty-six hours after leaving Bangkok the train rolled into Nakon Lampang, one of the largest native towns of the north and the headquarters of the British teak firms operating under Siamese Government licence. My Forest Manager, who was to be my boss, met me and took me to his comfortable compound. There he regarded me gravely, and I felt that he was about to put to me a question of some importance. What was it to be? My opinion of Jutland? My impressions of Siam?

"Can you play bridge?" was what he actually asked.

I shook my head.

"Then you'll have to learn. Not often that fellows out in the jungle *do* meet, but sometimes as many as four get together, and then it's darned hard luck on the other three if the fourth can't play. They soon get sick of talking to one another, you see."

And so for a month I remained in Nakon, learning—rather unsuccessfully, I fear—how to play bridge. I also learnt, or began to learn, the language.

In this I wasn't particularly helped by the mission

Lao grammar and dictionary being printed in Lao characters. Thus, if one was to learn Lao, one had to know a certain amount of the language to begin with, so to speak. However, with the aid of my newly-acquired boy and of the Forest Manager, I managed to make some headway.

The Lao language, which is very similar to Siamese except for the writing, which is entirely different and more like Burmese, comes by no means easily to the European. Being monosyllabic, it has to make up for lack of variety by means of " tones," and " tones " to the average white man presented extraordinary difficulty. There were eight of these tones: the High Explosive, the Low Explosive, the Rising, the Falling, the Acute, the Common, the Distressed, and one other the name of which I forget. And, according to whichever tone was used in connection with a word, so did that word possess a distinct and separate meaning.

For example:

*Mah* (as in car). If in the rising tone, as though one were going to ask a question, it meant " dog." If in the common tone, it meant " to come." If spoken in a low, explosive sort of way, as though one had turned suddenly angry, it meant " a horse." And so on.

As if the tones were not enough, there were added complications as exemplified by the word " kow," which had four variations of pronunciation. There was " kow," spoken very short and sharp. There was " kaouw," dragged out. There was " khow," aspirated and short. And there was " khaouw," aspirated and long drawn out. Then multiply these four by the eight varieties of tones, and you had no less than thirty-two possible meanings to the one word " kow " according to the combination of tone and pronunciation. This is an extreme instance, but almost every word in the Lao language was capable of at least two or three different interpretations, though to the natives the different tones made different *words* in themselves.

Personally, I never could get the tones right, and most Europeans agreed that one had to be bred and born in Siam to master them. The resultant mistakes we were wont to make were ridiculous; *seea*, for instance, meant " coat " or " tiger " according to tone, and on cold weather evenings I must often have called to my boy for him to bring me my warm tiger. The word " khai," too, meant either far or near according to tone; thus if one met a villager and asked him whether such-and-such a place was " near," one might be saying " far " for all one knew and his answer would thus be meaningless either way. And on one occasion I remember a friend of mine shouting for his boots very late at night and wondering why the " boy " was so long in bringing them. He found out when eventually the cook appeared, looking somewhat sullen after having been dragged out of his bed at the other end of the town !

I also bought a pony during my stay in Nakon, the law of the firm being that each forest assistant should possess at least two ponies for getting about on. Most of the dealers in the district were Shans, and as there was a scarcity in horse-flesh that season I hadn't much to choose from ; several wretched specimens were led past me, but eventually a light chestnut of very pleasing appearance was produced, so pleasing that I wondered what the snag about him was.

" I'll let my pony-boy ride him up and down the lane," said the Forest Manager, who was with me at the time.

The pony-boy mounted and put the animal through his paces. Everything seemed all right. I then mounted and, clutching wildly at reins and saddle pommel—which was all I knew about riding—shot up to the market-place and back. Again the brute seemed perfectly well-behaved and tractable. So I bought him on the spot and named him Sunstar. Later both myself and others were to call him the Yellow Peril, but of that more anon. . . .

It was on a pouring morning in early August that I first set out into the wilds to join Orwell, who was one of our senior forest assistants in charge of the Muang Ngow forest four days' march from Nakon. Mounted on Sunstar, and with two baggage elephants carrying the tent and camp furniture I was to use in the future, plus half a dozen coolies carrying the lighter articles of my kit, I moved out of the town and began crossing the plain, beyond which the jungle hills rose tier upon tier till their cloud-swathed crests cut the sky-line. My mahouts and coolies knew the way blindfold, the F. M. had told me, as well as each stage of the journey and where to sleep. I therefore had nothing to do but jog along on my pony at the same pace as the elephants and coolies.

The first day's march was the shortest—a bare ten miles—but before reaching the village of Sadet, where we were to camp, the river Mae Wang had to be crossed, and we found it in semi-flood. The elephants took the river first, and mighty fine it was to see and hear their great legs threshing through the surging, yellow water. Sunstar was then unsaddled and towed across by my pony-boy, and then I and the coolies struggled over, half-wading and half-swimming.

Having reached the village, the party made directly for its temple, which was surrounded by the usual compound and outhouses. To my astonishment my camp furniture was taken right into the temple itself and my bed set up directly in front of the great bronze Buddha on its pedestal. I glanced somewhat fearfully at a yellow-robed priest and his novices who were watching the proceedings, but they merely smiled amiably at me and appeared to take the whole thing as a matter of course; at which it dawned on me that nowhere in the world could religion be more tolerant and more kindly than in Siam.

A lantern on the table, I had my supper beneath the bronze Buddha. Overhead little tinsel ornaments suspended from the roof caught high lights from the lantern and tinkled softly in the breeze. From the outhouses came the faint murmur of my men. The rain had ceased, and with the coming of night peace wrapped the world in gentle darkness.

The meal over, I lit a cigarette and strolled out of the temple compound. From the village drifted the laughter of brown maidens, and in between the sighing of the peepul tree overhead I could hear the ruminative munch of my tethered elephants eating their fodder. And, as I stood there under the calm night, I rubbed my eyes and wondered whether I were dreaming. *Surely* I was no longer in the twentieth

century! Had I not this very day forded rivers
without the aid of bridges, ridden a pony instead of
reclining in a motor-car, and in place of a hotel was
not my resting-place a bed set in an Eastern temple
beneath an Eastern image? I turned, retraced my
steps through the compound, and, still with a strong
sense of unreality, extinguished the lantern and crept
through my mosquito net.

The next day we struck a cart-road winding between
forest, and for fifteen miles, mostly through knee-deep
mud in which riding was almost impossible, we followed
it. It rained dismally and the attentions of horse-
flies and mosquitoes were ceaseless, yet when we
finally camped in a little bamboo shanty built for
the use of the company's employees in a clearing by
the side of the road, I was supremely, idiotically
happy. I had travelled instead of merely arriving.

I was to journey along that fifty-two-mile road from
Nakon to Muang Ngow on many occasions: in heat
and in shadow, in rain and in mist, in sickness and
in health; yet I never ceased from loving it. I loved
its grandeur where it climbed up through the great
portals of rock guarding the pass leading down into
the Mae Ngow watershed, portals where monkeys
whooed and the panther coughed raggedly; I loved
its little villages dotted along its length; I loved
the little streams one encountered every few miles;
I loved even its long stretches of mud in the rainy
season. Ah, you who flash along in motor-cars, you
cannot guess at the joys of travelling along a lonely
road with pony and elephants.

On the fourth morning after leaving Nakon we
struck paddy-fields. On the further side of them we

forded a yellow, swirling river, the Mae Ngow river. The little village of Muang Ngow lay along the opposite bank, and riding slowly between the rows of shanties and market stalls I came to the Muang Ngow Forest compound of the company.

A powerfully-built man in khaki shorts, white shirt and white topee, with a big, very clean-shaven face, advanced to meet me.

" Orwell, I presume."

Stanley was greeting Livingstone !

## CHAPTER THREE

## ELEPHANTS AND MUD-SORES

FOR three weeks I toured round Orwell's forest in company with Orwell himself. Every night we made camp in a different spot amidst the rolling, jungle-clad hills, and by the end of this period I had digested as much of this remarkable new work as was possible for an ex-naval officer.

Briefly, Orwell's forest consisted of the whole of the basin (or watershed) of the river Mae Ngow and its numerous tributaries. From the sources of the Mae Ngow to where it ran out into its parent river, the Mae Yome, was a distance of a little over thirty miles, while in places its tributaries extended for twenty miles to right and left. Thus the total area under Orwell was not far short of one thousand square miles, a no mean responsibility.

The lower half of the Mae Ngow basin was closed for afforestation purposes when I arrived, but the top half, which was open, had contained originally about a hundred thousand marketable teak trees, all of which were being gradually felled, logged, measured, hammered and then dragged down to the Mae Ngow river for " ounging " into the big main river Mae Yome by elephant. Once, I learnt, the logs had reached the Mae Yome, they would float more or less unattended down to the rafting stations some two hundred miles to the south, where they would be

ON THE MARCH.

made up into rafts before completing the final three-hundred-mile journey to the saw-mills of Bangkok. The average time, I gathered from Orwell, it took for a log to reach Bangkok after being placed in the Mae Ngow was five years.

Here is a rough map showing what is meant by the Mae Ngow watershed:

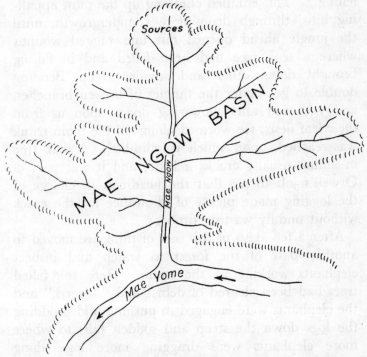

Dealing with such an immense amount of timber, the extraction had to be done gradually and spread over a number of years. Orwell's method was to " work " first one tributary and then another. Not till all the teak growing round one particular side-creek of the Mae Ngow had been dragged into the

c

parent stream did he start felling in the next; in the same way, not till the first batch had floated down the Mae Ngow and out into the Mae Yome did he start placing any more logs in from the second tributary, otherwise hopeless jams would speedily have formed.

The first job Orwell showed me was " inspecting felling." This entailed climbing up the most appalling hills, through dripping wet undergrowth, until the jungle ahead opened out into ragged wounds where a teak tree had been felled and in falling brought down other and smaller trees. Bending double to get under the tangles of broken branches, and with red ants showering down upon us from their leaf nests, we wormed along till the main trunk was reached, upon which we climbed. A teak tree in falling usually cracks a little, and it was part of Orwell's job to see that the headman in charge of the logging made plenty of allowance for the crack without unduly wasting timber.

After a few days of this sort of thing we moved to another part of the forest to watch and inspect elephants working at the stump. Here the felled trees had been cleared of debris and " logged," and the elephants were engaged in pushing and prodding the logs down the steep and sodden hills to where more elephants were dragging more logs along specially constructed paths. The elephants, I gathered from Orwell, lived almost natural lives in their natural surroundings, working only a few hours a day and then being hobbled to rest and graze at will in the jungle. I will devote a chapter to elephants later, but here let me say that there can be no animal of more absorbing interest and fascination. To the ordinary man in the street at home an elephant is perhaps rather a comical creature, one about which he thinks in Circus terms and as giving rides to children at the Zoo; in reality, however, he does not know what an elephant looks like, for he has only seen few placid females. A great tusker in its own surroundings resembles them no more than a heavy-weight boxing champion resembles some fat little woman.

After inspecting at the stump we moved down one of the numerous cart-roads till we came out on to the bank of the Mae Ngow. On an open space by the river were more logs, neatly arranged in rows and ready to be measured and hammered. With gangs of coolies in attendance, each man carrying a heavy timber-stamping hammer, Orwell then went up and down the rows, classifying the logs according to quality, and recording their sizes in a notebook.

There were four kinds of hammers, all of which had to be imprinted on every single log. Firstly, the one bearing the initials of the company; secondly, the one giving the year number; thirdly, the one giving the assistant's number, and, lastly, the one denoting the classification—first, second or third class. Thus, on a log reaching Bangkok, those in the saw-mill could tell at a glance its quality, the name of the forest assistant who had classified it, and the year it had been put into the jungle stream.

When the logs had all been hammered, more elephants—Orwell had one hundred and eighty under him—came on the scene and rolled them down the bank into the river-bed, where they would await the next " floating rise."

By this time I was beginning to become painfully aware of the numerous pests that inhabit the jungle in the rains. First and foremost were the mosquitoes, which all day long plastered the bare portions of one's anatomy, never allowing a moment's rest from scratching. There were two chief types of mosquito. The commonest were large fellows with striped legs who could give you dengue fever but not malaria. Then there were little, brown, harmless-looking chaps who came out only in the evening and who stood on their heads when biting you; these were the dreaded anopheles, the females of which could give you malaria but not dengue. To guard against their attentions we teak-wallahs were in the habit of taking five or ten grains of quinine every day in the rains.

There was also a third type of mosquito, which I did not see till I had been in the country a year. But then I got a shock, for veritably it was The Mosquito of All Mosquitoes, standing as it did a good inch high. This may sound an exaggeration, but is literally true, for I saw a good many of them; they always went singly, and were usually buzzing round a standing teak tree. On the first occasion I came upon one I bolted incontinently, but having been reassured by my coolies that the giant type didn't bite, was able to examine later some specimens at leisure. They were perfect mosquitoes down to the last detail, only at least twenty times the size of the largest of other types. They were of a negative, black-brown colour, without stripes to the legs or any particular distinctive feature, and I often wonder whether they are known to science.

Then there were leeches, my " betes noires," quite

literally. These looped along the ground when they smelt you, waving their disgusting, sightless heads to get their direction, then wormed their smooth, thin, black bodies through the lace-holes of your jungle-boots and, fastening on as you walked along unsuspectingly, fed to repletion. They also had an unpleasant habit of dropping off branches down your neck. Evergreen jungle was where they were usually encountered, and as Orwell and I in our rounds passed through a good deal of this, we were never free for long from the atrocities. I don't know whether, being just out from home, I smelt fresher than my companion, but I do know that for every leech he got I got ten. When I arrived back in camp my boots were squelching in ·blood, and on taking off my shirt, great round, red patches showed in the drab khaki. The loathsome things, the shape of slugs now that they were full-fed, were completely torpid, and I had great pleasure in burning them to death with matches.

Sweat-bees there were, innocuous little creatures in themselves, but all the more irritating for that. " In the sweat of thy face shalt thou eat bread." Never had that phrase been borne in upon me more than in the teak forest. For work out there *was* sweating; one rained sweat continuously, and the " sweat-bee " liked it. He was a pale, short, fat bee without a sting, and was so helplessly slow and clumsy in his movements that when he alighted on you, you hadn't the heart to kill him. Mosquitoes and flies, being quick on the uptake, had a sporting chance and were therefore fair game, but the " sweat-bee " was such a pathetic little person that you had to let him crawl about unharmed, as a result of which you endured agonies of tickling.

Which brings us to ticks. These—tiny, round things, with myriads of tiny legs and a shell-like back —fastened on you unawares, preferably on the chest or in the armpits, and fed till they swelled after the manner of the leeches. The trouble then was to get them off; they were too small for you to burn without singeing yourself, while if you tried to pluck them off they left their heads behind, thereby setting up an irritation that was simply maddening.

Sand-flies were another joy. They flourished near elephant camps, and usually came to the attack just as you were dropping off to sleep. Being very small, they easily passed through the holes in the mosquito net and, settling in your hair, bit your scalp until you well-nigh screamed. One teak-wallah was so plagued with them that he thought if he were supplied with a very closely woven mosquito net he would rest in peace, even if he *were* a trifle short of breath through lack of ventilation; so he wrote to a firm of outfitters in Bangkok asking them to send him a very " fine " net. And he got one. It had cupids on the top, pink and blue ribbons at the corners, cherubs—but why go on? He had been supplied with a bridal mosquito net instead of the sort he wanted.

Of course there were ants, the carroty-red ones that fell on to you from bushes and stabbed you as though with red-hot needles, being the worst. Then there were huge solitary black ants, like the huge solitary mosquitoes I have mentioned: not quite such freaks, perhaps, but they bit—goodness how they bit! One bit my big toe as, bare-footed, I was crossing the split bamboo flooring of one of our jungle shanties, and the toe swelled up to such an extent that I couldn't get my boot on next morning. Then there were the tiniest of ants which, if you had any sort of hair lotion on, climbed up the legs of the bed and bit your scalp like the sand-flies. The way to compete with these was to stand the legs of the bed in saucers filled with kerosene.

By the time we had returned to Orwell's compound and the luxury of bungalows, I was beginning to suffer severely from mud-sores, a common complaint of teak-wallahs. In my case the sores were caused by the leech-bites festering through my having constantly to wade through mud and filthy water; there also seemed to be very little healing power in the damp, hot air of the jungle itself. I had been supplied with a medicine-chest, and I washed the places, which were mainly on shins and ankles, with permanganate of potash, then dressed them with lint, and hoped for the best.

The morning after our arrival back in the compound, Orwell strode into my room round about six o'clock, and I raised a sleepy head.

" Come on! " he shouted. " A mahout's just reported that one of our elephants has died suddenly at . . ." he mentioned a locality six miles away, " and we've got to go out and inspect the body. I've ordered your pony-boy to saddle Sunstar, and we'll ride there."

I hastily pulled on my kit and rushed out into the compound. During the previous three weeks' tour of the forest neither of us had ridden our ponies, as the going had been far too steep and rough, but now their use was apparent. Orwell had a grey mare, a brute of an animal, with the devil in her eye and hooves that were best avoided. If you went too close to her she rushed at you open-mouthed, being a regular killer, but she was as swift as a swallow, and when later I saw Orwell play polo on her the pair made a magnificent sight.

The mare was already saddled and standing by the compound gates, and so was Sunstar. When I reached him, however, he proved a very different animal from the one on which I had ridden out from Nakon; he was circling round and round my pony-boy, who was holding the reins, and when I neared to mount him he rose up on his hind-legs in true Far Western style; at which I, who was no Buck Jones, stroked my chin and regarded him dubiously.

"Excitement," said Orwell, with that irritating calmness of good riders. "Excitement at being with another pony. He'll soon get over it."

He certainly showed no signs of doing so now. But with the courage of despair I made a grab at him and flung myself on his back. Next second total darkness descended on me as Sunstar shot forward like a catapult with a jerk that brought my topee down over my face.

My left hand grasped the reins; my right the pommel of the saddle, which was still all I knew about riding. If I let go of either to remove the topee so unaccountably jammed over my eyes, I should fall off. And I did not want to fall off.

A queer feeling, rushing along at a good many miles per hour on horseback without being able to see a thing, and one that I don't wish to have repeated.

Luckily the topee suddenly slipped off of its own accord, and I found I was careering madly down the street of the little village. Ahead of me men, women, children, pariahs, pigs and hens were spraying out of my way like flying-fish fanning out before the bows of a ship, but providentially all got clear of me in time and I reached the end of the village without killing anyone. Finally, the waters of the Mae Ngow river, which ran across the road below the hamlet, brought Sunstar up short, and a few seconds later Orwell flashed up anxiously on the grey mare.

We turned and together rode back through the village and then along the six miles of cart-road that separated us from the elephant casualty. Every inch of those miles provided an agonising jolt as I endeavoured to restrain Sunstar from breaking out again into a mad gallop; indeed, the journey was only made at all possible through Orwell keeping his own mare at a walking pace (months later I discovered that Sunstar had been a racing pony in his youth, with the result that he had become imbued with the idea that any pony in sight must at once be passed at full speed!).

I never thought I'd live to be thankful to see a dead elephant, but when at last the carcass hove in sight in a clearing on one side of the road, I dismounted with a sigh of relief. I soon forgot my own small troubles, however, at the pathos of the huge, still body. On the great head was a tiny blue forest flower, placed there by the mahout to speed the parting spirit, and the brown man himself was there, looking sad and slightly frightened. He salaamed to Orwell and began talking rapidly to him in Lao, every now and then pointing to the ground in different parts of the clearing.

" He's saying," Orwell explained to me, " that the elephant was perfectly well yesterday evening, but that it had lain down and got up again a good many times during the night. Must have been in awful pain, poor brute. Come round with me and we'll have a look at the orifices. And take care of your hands. Don't touch any part of the body."

We went delicately round the huge mound of flesh, to see that the orifices were exuding blood. Orwell whistled :

" Anthrax," he said. " All the signs. Those cursed village cattle have been grazing here, I'll be bound. They're simply stiff with it." He glanced at his watch. " I'll ride back to the compound now at once. You can follow later. Got to send out orders for all other elephants in the district to be taken away, and to arrange for the body to be burnt. There's nothing more contagious than anthrax."

So the grey mare galloped off up the cart-road, raising fountains of mud behind her heels, and after a suitable interval I mounted Sunstar. He was still just as excitable as before, however, and in an instant was off hot-foot after the mare, I hanging on as best I could.

Somehow, in spite of mud-holes, sharp twists in the road, overhanging branches, and a dozen other different kinds of snags, I survived those nightmare six miles, only to meet disaster when in sight of safety. For Sunstar took the turning into the compound gates at such a speed that he ran into the fence, and I was thrown over his head, my face hitting, first the fence, and then the ground as I crashed down on to it. I must next have lost consciousness for half a minute or so.

When I came to I staggered to my feet, blood pouring from me. Sunstar—he became the Yellow Peril from that instant—was unconcernedly cropping the grass, and, staggering past him, I made my way shakily over the compound towards the office. Orwell, roused by shouts from some coolies who had noticed me, came running out, and soon I was lying flat in a long cane-chair with him and the boys sponging me with vinegar.

The results of that fall were a badly broken nose which, in the absence of any doctor, had to reset itself as best it could, a black eye and bruised cheekbone, and a lump on my forehead the size of an egg. These, together with the state of my legs, which were still covered with mud-sores, reduced me to a somewhat unpleasant-looking object.

And yet, as I lay on my bed that night listening to the rain on the roof, I still felt absurdly happy in my new surroundings.

## CHAPTER FOUR

# SOME JUNGLE JOURNEYS

IN the rainy season the Mae Ngow was usually at a level which, though high enough to fill the bed from bank to bank, did not quite provide sufficient water to float the teak logs resting on the sandy bottom. Every six weeks or so, I had gathered from Orwell, an exceptionally heavy downpour would turn the Mae Ngow into a band of yellow, swirling water deep enough to float the heaviest log. These rises apparently rarely lasted for more than a few hours, so it was very important that the elephants should stop the timber stacking at treacherous, rock-strewn corners; in other words, the timber had to be kept moving continuously if full advantage were to be taken of every precious minute of the rise. One of these rises occurred a day or two after my fall and, mounted on a placid old bull elephant, I went out to see Orwell directing operations from the back of another.

Is there any spectacle, I wonder, that can surpass in magnificence the sight of twenty or thirty elephants, all in the prime of condition, " ounging " timber down a swollen jungle stream? Crash! A great teak log collides with a rock head-on and swings round broadside to the current. The other end is caught by a jutting-out portion of the opposite bank, and the river is blocked from one side to the other. More

logs are riding down upon the first. Boom! Boom!
Hollow and sullen. A pile, a jam is forming. Four
tuskers down here, quick, roars Orwell. What's
that? The water's too deep? Nonsense. Get your
elephants *in*!

They're right under the stack now, having
approached it from below. Careful, warns the boss.
That's it, the key log! Poo Ten's tusks are under one
end of it, but what's wrong with Poo Luang? The
ends of his tusks are too sharp, and they're slipping
on the smooth surface! Orwell makes a note to cut
three inches off them this evening, orders Poo Koo
to take Poo Luang's place, then yells for them all to
lift together.

The key log moves, and a moment later the whole
stack dissolves with a crackling roar on top of mahouts
and elephants. See them now, Poo Ake, Poo Luang,
Poo Koo, Poo Ten, fighting for their lives in all the
grandeur of their strength. Huge as they are, they
lunge with lightning speed in order to splay the logs
apart; tusks flash, trunks shoot and curl, huge fore-
heads fend off great balks that would crush a man to
instant death, and the mass is flattened out and once
more on the move.

Leaving the four to guard that point, Orwell and I
urge our old tuskers five hundred yards up-stream.
Here more elephants are working. No stack has yet
formed, but the timber is coming down faster and
faster from the north, and the leviathans are finding
plenty to do in keeping the logs riding free of one
another.

The uproar as we go up and down the river is
terrific. The trumpeting and bellowing of elephants,

" swooshes " of collapsing portions of the bank, the crackling and booming of timber, yells of mahouts and chainmen, the thrumming of the stream—these and other sounds combine to make one great blare of noise. My ears are filled with a strange orchestra, my eyes with swift movement, while in my nostrils is the smell of moist earth and rain-blown wind. I have known what it is to be alive to-day.

By evening the rise was over. The Mae Ngow sank to its normal level, and the logs began to ground in the shallows. Yet Orwell expressed great satis-faction: a good three thousand logs, so he estimated, must have floated out into the main Mae Yome since morning, and the remaining timber had moved down well.

Next morning my legs had become worse through tramping about on the muddy banks when not actually riding on the tusker, and Orwell, who had planned taking me out on another jungle round, looked somewhat anxious.

" You'll have to lie up altogether," said he. " And if the places don't get better in a week or ten days, there's nothing for it but to go back to Nakon and see the missionary doctor."

And so, while Orwell went out on one of his periodical tours, I lay on a long cane-chair, reading two-months-old newspapers and the black-covered Lao grammar that was printed in Lao. When he got back my legs were just the same, no better and no worse, and though my bashed-in countenance had improved, he plumped for Nakon.

Personally, I loathed the idea of the new chum going back helplessly to H.Q. because, poor fellow, he'd actually had to spend a few weeks in the jungle! And Orwell, who like most brave men was a kind one, must have read my thoughts, for he said :

" Never mind. You'll soon get acclimatised. And, what's more, you'll know what to avoid in the future. One's riding Sunstar in the company of another pony, and the other's going through leech areas. And now about Nakon. As you're going in there, you might as well bring me back some specie. The balance in the strong-room's pretty low, and I'll want twenty thousand *ticals* at least."

Good, I reflected. My journey into Nakon wouldn't be an utter waste of time from the point of view of the Company.

" Do I ride an elephant in? " I queried.

" No," answered Orwell. " An elephant's darned uncomfortable for a long journey. Your pony 'll be all right on his own, and if you go at a walking pace you needn't disturb the bandages."

And so, on the Yellow Peril, the whole village turning out in the hopes of seeing me fall off a second time, again I faced the Muang Ngow–Nakon road. This time, however, no lamb could have been milder. He walked sedately past the disappointed villagers, breasted the Mae Ngow current at the ford with never an attempt to sit down in it, and when he came to the vast expanse of mud on the road beyond the paddy-fields he neither flinched nor jibbed; for mile after mile, with me on his back, he slowly pounded through that frightful morass, and long before we were half-way to the capital he had become Sunstar again to me. And indeed he *was* two personalities. In company he was the Yellow Peril, possessing every bad quality known to a horse. By himself in the jungle he was the perfect mount: nothing from an elephant to a leopard could scare him, yet withal he was as mild and obedient as any household dog.

On arrival in Nakon in a thick drizzle I learnt that the only other Campbell in the north, a teak-wallah like myself in another firm, had just died out in the wilds. He had been ailing for some days, apparently, and then, at last realising that something serious was the matter with him, had started for H.Q., at the same time sending his pony-boy on ahead with the news. Campbell's Forest Manager in Nakon, on receiving the message, then rushed out to meet him, leaving relays of stretcher-bearing coolies behind him at odd points on the muddy apology for a road. And on this road, still a long way from Nakon, he had met Campbell.

Campbell, he found, had typhoid, and though he urged the coolies along as fast as they could go, the sick man never reached Nakon; he died in camp, the rain pattering on the tent and the lonely jungle all round, after making a temporary rally in which he had talked of the prospects of the coming polo in the inter-company Christmas matches. And now the Manager (himself dead of fever since) was back again in H.Q., looking older than before.

It was during this stay of mine in Nakon, while under the care of the mission doctor, that I heard another grim story *à propos* of the specie I was getting ready to take back with me along the jungle-fringed road to Muang Ngow. The story concerned two teak-wallahs who a few years back had been attacked

STACK OF TEAK LOGS JUST FORMING ON FALLING WATERS.

by dacoits when taking specie out to their forests, and this is how I was told it.

A jungle night in the cold weather. A log fire, piled up between two tents in a clearing, burns merrily, the flames flickering and sending leaping shadows over the trees. In the tents, round two camp beds, the square boxes of specie lie as they have been placed by the coolies who have unloaded the baggage elephants that evening.

At a table, near the fire, two teak-wallahs are seated peacefully; happily tired after travelling all day through jungle behind their specie-carrying elephants, they are reading by the light of lanterns placed on the table. Smoke from their pipes rises in the air and mingles with the scented smoke of the log fire. Every now and then a gust of cold-weather wind surges through the forest, sending cascades of sparks streaking out into the gloom.

Crash! A volley tears the night apart with hideous clamour. A., who has been reading peacefully, slides stupidly off his chair on to the ground, where he lies motionless. B., wounded in the arm, jumps to his feet, glares round him, rushes to the tent where the specie is, and seizes his revolver.

In their leaf shelters near by, the coolies, servants and mahouts of the two white men crouch and shiver; armed desperadoes have encircled the camp and to resist is asking for death.

In the deep shadows of the jungle surrounding the clearing stand four evil men, smoking guns of an ancient type in their hands. One of the white men is dead—have they not just run in and mauled him horribly in order to make assurance doubly sure?—

D

but there still remains one alive and obviously intent on defending the money for which they have come. They stand for a short while undecided. They are four to one, yet their souls are craven, and now that they have done murder their weapons shake. Suddenly one bolts, and the others follow him.

B., one arm useless at his side, rushes back across the clearing and, grief-stricken and horror-struck, bends over his mutilated friend. . . .

MURDER. Swiftly the word runs through the jungle. A white man has been murdered. The word reaches the Siamese authorities, and presently sturdy little Siamese gendarmes, skilfully led, are combing the villages. The four are tracked, and eventually cornered. There is a fight, one of the dacoits is killed, two are captured, and the fourth escapes into the jungle.

After a trial the captured pair are executed. This leaves only the fourth, who is trying to reach the border and cross over to Annam, for no Siamese village will shelter him.

A great tiger slinking through the undergrowth. He has failed in a kill, and is hungry and vicious. He hears something coming noisily along, and flattens. Nearer and nearer draw the sounds, the tiger springs, and life for the fourth dacoit ends in a choking scream. A few trinkets and shreds of clothing on a lonely jungle path are all that is left to tell the tale to some gendarmes who happen along later.

Thus passed the four murderers of A., teak-wallah.

After that it was decreed that whenever possible teak-wallahs should be accompanied by a gendarmerie escort when taking specie out to their forests, and so it was with four of these brown, smiling little police-men that I set out on the return journey to Muang Ngow. I rode immediately behind the two elephants that were carrying the boxes, while the gendarmes walked on either side of them with rifles across their shoulders; even then it occurred to me that we could easily have been ambushed, for thick jungle bordered the road continuously.

By night I slept with the specie boxes all round my bed, and with the automatic pistol I had brought out from England beneath the thin camp mattress on a level with my thigh. The weapon was easier to get at in that position than if it had been under the pillow, and there was the added reason that if it went off accidentally it wouldn't blow my brain-pan to smithereens.

On arrival at Muang Ngow, Orwell informed me that I was to leave only half the specie with him, as he had had a note from Swan, the man in charge of the company's most remote forest, saying that he also was very short of cash. I and my transport could have one day's rest, Orwell said, after which I was to take on the remaining boxes and deliver them to Swan.

And so, in shrouds of rain, off I started on an entirely new sixty-mile cross-country journey from Muang Ngow to Pohng, the place where Swan had his H.Q. near the Indo-Chinese border. After traversing the wildest territory, threaded by rock-strewn rivers and mantled with very thick jungle, I arrived at my destination safely and turned over the money to Swan. When finally I got back to Muang Ngow I had completed, in one month, some two hundred and twenty-five miles of jungle travel in the height of the rains and therefore in dreadful conditions, yet surprisingly enough my mud-sores were all healed and I was conscious of feeling extremely well. I also had the satisfaction of knowing I loved the life.

There followed a month of miscellaneous jobs for me round the upper part of the Mae Ngow river, jobs that I felt instinctively were only given me for the sake of increasing my knowledge of the language and of jungle ways in general, and then, when the rains were over and the lovely cold weather was just beginning, Orwell sent for me to return to the compound.

I found him in the office, bending over a large-scale map of the whole of the Muang Ngow forest.

" Got a proper job of work for you at last," said he. He pointed to a portion of the closed area. " The Forest Department have been girdling the Mae Lah basin here, and you're to inspect their girdling on our behalf to see that they're not missing any valuable trees. You're also to make full maps and give us detailed reports of the area. I'll come out with you first to the Mae Lah and teach you a bit about gird-ling, and then leave you by yourself for several months."

I was delighted. At last!—a real job on my own and of my own, and a real jungle valley to myself.

## CHAPTER FIVE

# I BECOME SNAKE-CONSCIOUS

I STOOD before my tent in the brief twilight of the tropical evening. For the last week Orwell had been showing me round the valley and teaching me how to inspect girdling, and now I was alone. The rains being well over, the wind that sighed through the forest trees was pleasantly cool; above the camp clearing the sky was an egg-shell blue, devoid of any cloud; at the base of the clearing the little Mae Lah river tinkled, its waters limpid after the muddy turbulence of the rains; to the left smoke rose quietly from the fires of my brown Lao servants, coolies and mahouts; somewhere in the rear the bells of my two baggage elephants clocked, and ever and anon I could hear a crackling and snapping as the placid creatures browsed on the overhanging vegetation.

I had had my evening sluice in the tin bath at the rear of the tent, and now was clad in cotton singlet and wide-bottomed Chinese trousers in place of the khaki jungle kit I wore by day. Slipping a sweater over the singlet, for the chill in the air was increasing with the dipping of the sun, I sauntered over the clearing to the side of the Mae Lah river. There I summoned to me my friends—those good chaps in the navy with whom I had served during the War that now seemed so long ago.

They came, those phantom friends, and to them I

talked. I said to them: "Didn't expect to see me here, did you, right in the middle of a teak forest? Nice little spot, don't you think?" And they at once agreed with me. That was the best of phantom friends; they never argued, and always said exactly what you wanted them to.

Standing there by the cool tinkling stream in the gloaming, I related quite a lot about myself and my experiences; I told my friends—old Gibbs who was always late for breakfast in the wardroom; Jones, the snottie, who had been such a terror at playing pranks with one's hammock; Smith, the young two-striper who *would* sing Gilbert and Sullivan in his bath—I told them all about my wonderful two-hundred-and-twenty-five-mile journey through the jungle in the rains, I showed them my pony Sunstar and put him through his various paces, and finally I gave them a personally conducted tour round the whole of the Mae Ngow basin, whereupon they expressed themselves vastly impressed.

Some of my coolies and servants were doubtless casting curious eyes upon me as I talked and gesticulated there by the stream with my invisible friends, but I did not mind in the least; for these gentle Laos were living examples of respect; had I stood on my head and sung the Dream of Gerontius right through they would not have turned a hair.

Night swept a giant hand over the valley, the valley that was mine. I walked over to my tent, wherein a Hitchcock lamp shone cheerfully on a table, and sat down in my camp chair. My boy brought the evening peg of whisky, and as I sipped it I glanced round in comfortable satisfaction. Free at last from the maddening attentions of mosquitoes and other pests of the rains, sane in mind and body, I was able to enjoy detail.

Behind the chair my bed glimmered under the white mosquito net; behind that was the " bathroom," which consisted merely of the space between the inner cover and the outer cover of the tent at the back; beneath the bed, chained to one of the legs according to Company rules, rested the padlocked wooden box in which were kept my pistol, ready cash and other odds and ends; on the side of the tent opposite to the bed was a battered suit-case containing my changes of clothes—shirts, shorts, puttees, Chinese trousers and singlets; in the centre of the verandah of the tent, where I was at the moment, stood chair, stool and table; on the right of it were the " hahps " (baskets carried by my coolies when on the march) containing stores in the shape of tinned foods, sugar, bottles and the like; and, lastly, on the left of the verandah reposed the two empty howdahs of my baggage elephants.

Seven o'clock. I call for dinner, which, although I am miles and miles away from any kind of civilisation, will consist of four courses; if one is to do hard work one must eat well, being one of my Forest Manager's mottoes. The boy appears, sets the table, vanishes, then reappears with a plate of chicken soup. Next come rissoles, also made of chicken. The joint is chicken again, tough, stringy jungle chicken roasted in pigs' fat, and the last course is caramel custard. An hour after finishing the meal I turn in, to fall almost immediately asleep to the sighing of the trees enclosing the little camp.

A grey dawn filters through the teak forest. The glimmer increases, becomes light, and the stream, the forest greenery, the rare jungle flowers, take on hues. I peer through the mosquito net and shout to my boy, who, bare-footed, crosses the clearing from the servants' shelter carrying some water—a kettle of hot and a pail of cold from the running stream. I sluice myself down in the tin bath in the " bath-room," first handling my yellow sponge gingerly, for a tiny yellow scorpion may be lurking in it; this happened to another teak-wallah, so I have been told, as a result of which he nearly lost the sight of one eye.

I dress quickly in boots, wing-screw-caulked to gain a hold on the steep and slippery hills, puttees, khaki shorts, vest for soaking up the sweat, and khaki shirt. Breakfast: two small boiled eggs from the nearest village, bread made by the cook, tinned, runny butter, coffee strained through an old sock of mine, marmalade. I then put on my topee, grasp stick, pencil and girdling note-book, and after shouting to my head coolie, stride out of the clearing to my new work.

We walk silently in Indian file through the forest towards the last tree inspected the previous day by Orwell and myself. This was numbered 742, and I must therefore find tree No. 743. My head coolie with tape measure goes first, then I, then a coolie carrying a porous, red, earthenware jar containing my filtered drinking-water, then another coolie carrying my cold lunch, then a coolie carrying the few simple belongings of the head coolie and the others, and the rear is brought up by yet another coolie who seems to have tacked himself on to the party for no reason known to himself or to anyone else. We steal along like ghosts through the dew-drenched forest, the men's bare feet making no sound and I instinctively walking as silently as possible to copy them. Only the " whoo " of monkeys can be heard and the occasional chatter and screech of green parrakeets and " did-you-do-it " plovers.

Somewhere in the riot of jungle hills tossing all round us is teak tree No. 743. *And with very little hesitation we go straight up to it.* It sounds difficult, but it's all a matter of obeying one simple rule : when in hilly country never *cross* even the smallest of water-sheds ; instead, follow round each fold in the ground, and not only will you never be lost, but you need never miss a single teak tree if you keep your eyes open. (In flat country, of course, it is much more difficult to keep one's whereabouts clear, and one has to rely almost entirely on the coolies' jungle-sense.)

I pause before tree No. 743. On it is a blaze, with the number and size of the girth written in the blaze by the Forest Department party that has preceded me. At a height of about three feet above the base the tree has been girdled ; that is to say, the sap-wood has been cut away till the ruddy-brown heart-wood is showing all round. (A teak tree will not float when green, consequently it has to be girdled, or killed, and then left standing at least two years, by the end of which time it will be dry and buoyant enough to place in the river.) I take a note in my book of the number, size and marketable quality of the tree, then, after glancing round to get my bearings and the line on which the F.D. party has worked, move on through the jungle intent on spying out more teak trees. Here and there I discover that the party has missed girdling a tree not purposely left untouched as a " seed-bearer," but in the main the work has been excellently done, and my own work is chiefly confined to making notes and maps of the locality with a view to facilitating the extraction of the timber later on.

Round about noon I halt and, sitting on a tree blown down by the wind, eat my cold, somewhat unappetising tiffin of everlasting chicken. I have half an hour's rest afterwards, but sitting in sweat-stained clothing is none too pleasant, and I am glad to move on again. Not much work is done in the afternoon, however, for both I and the coolies now begin to tire rapidly, and by four o'clock I am back in my tent.

I wash the sweat and filth of the day off me, have tea, read, enter up my diary, eat my dinner, fight against sleep for an hour so as not to go to bed on a full stomach, then turn in and sleep like a log.

.      .      .      .      .

Thus passed the first of many days, varied only by Sundays, when I stayed in my tent and worked at reports and maps, and wrote up the diary required by company rules.

Monotony? Strangely enough, there was very little. The apparent sameness of the work held infinite variety. There was variety in the Mae Lah jungle itself, for instance, which in parts was evergreen and in parts bamboo, both giant and dwarf, while occasionally one came across great stretches of waist-high, sweet-smelling grass that were a joy to see and traverse; indeed, each separate, tiny side-creek of the Mae Lah contained different types of scents and sights.

I began to get acquainted with the inhabitants of the valley, the birds and the beasts. Though the majority of the latter remained unseen to me, I felt their presence there, almost penetrated their thoughts.

Firstly, there was the great tiger who used the path along the Mae Lah stream as he made his nightly prowls for food. Hardly a week went by without my seeing his pug-marks on the sand by the water, and his droppings. At times they were remarkably close to my camp, but somehow I never feared him greatly; he was a *sahib*, I was certain, and provided he wasn't annoyed would do one no harm.

Then there was the panther, whose coughing snarl I sometimes heard near the camp. One evening he chased a barking-deer right past my tent. I was just finishing tea, when a loud crashing in the under-growth behind me indicated that something out of the ordinary was happening; jungle animals, with the sole exception of the bear, move quietly unless very much alarmed, and on my rushing out of the tent to discover the cause of the noise, I almost collided with a barking-deer. The little animal, obviously in an ecstasy of terror, swerved past me, going all out, and, after nearly knocking over my astonished cook, disappeared into the jungle on the further bank of the Mae Lah.

As for me, I let forth a yell that would have startled the devil himself, for the faintest of movements had come from a patch of long grass out of which the deer had burst; one of the carnivora had evidently been after that deer and might at any moment mistake me for it!

When the echoes of my voice died away, the movement in the grass also ceased, and I listened intently. Was *it* also listening as it crouched there with flattened ears and snarling mouth?

I broke the ensuing silence to summon my coolies. In those days I hadn't a gun, and with drawn knives and yelling voices we all advanced towards the ambush in which the would-be slayer lurked. At the edge of it a strong " tom-cat " smell assailed our nostrils, a most creepy experience. Needless to say this spurred us to even louder shouts, whereupon a slight, almost imperceptible wave receded through the grass, and we knew that the cat was departing.

" *Seea dao*," said the coolies, " *seea dao*." Which told me that a " star tiger," or panther, had been within a few yards of us.

That night I welcomed the lamp and the whirring tick of the machinery inside it that kept the flame burning steadily without a chimney. Somewhere out in the gloom the " star tiger " was in all probability still slinking unappeased; but I had the comfort that at any rate the barking-deer was saved.

It was about this time that my chickens began to disappear one after another at night. My cook kept the wretched birds, with which he fed me equally wretchedly, in a fenced-off place near his tent at one end of the clearing, and I suspected the panther. He said, however, " No. It is not the panther, master. It is a . . ." and he spoke a Lao word of which I did not know the meaning. " If," he went on, " master will give me some rope, I will make a trap for it."

Sunstar was with me in the camp—the coolies had run up a bamboo stockade for him—and I gave the cook a length of his headstall rope. The cook then proceeded to rig up the most Heath Robinson sort of snare imaginable.

" You'll never catch anything with that," I told him.

" The master wait until morning, and then he see," was the confident reply. " The . . ." (unknown animal) " walk along here, master, and put his head into this noose. Then he jump at a chicken, the noose go tight, and he strangle himself."

" Very obliging of him, I'm sure," I answered in disbelief.

But that dusky gentleman was right, for next morning, wearing a grin which stretched from ear to ear, he appeared at the threshold of my tent with a perfect specimen of one of the most beautiful animals in the jungle—a leopard-cat. A leopard-cat (which is not to be confused with a civet-cat) is marked like a miniature leopard or panther (the terms are synonymous), but its body is rather more dog-like, for it stands straighter and taller than the average feline. This particular specimen had been strangled right enough by the noose, so it wasn't in the least disfigured and I had it skinned by the coolies. After that morning we lost no more chickens.

Then there was the lordly sambhur who sometimes flashed past me in his peerless stride as I waded through the waving jungle grass intent on teak. He was always alone, and I gathered from the more observant of the coolies that he clung to the valley with all the single-minded passion of his race. Being a sambhur, he had nothing in common with the smaller kinds of deer; they apparently moved from one locality to another as the mood took them, but he remained in the particular strip of territory he had made his own, fighting, I was sure, any other sambhur who tried to oust him; indeed, at times I heard his great challenge, which was never answered, echoing through the glens. He had nothing to fear from either the tiger or the panther, being too swift for the former and too well provided with weapons in the shape of antlers and hooves for the latter.

Then there were the bears, of which the valley seemed to be full. Their tracks were everywhere, and once I came across marks on the ground where the branch of a tree had broken beneath the weight of two and sent them crashing to earth. Which at first struck me as curious; this sort of thing might be expected to happen to human beings, but not to animals in their natural surroundings. Who ever heard of a cat falling off a tree or of a deer getting entangled in a thicket?

But then the bear is a fool, I reflected, after listening to the explanations of my coolies concerning the marks; he is in the jungle but not of it, blundering about and generally making an idiot of himself. The consequence is that to humans he is, though quite unintentionally, the most dangerous animal of the forest. Others, the tiger and the panther, for instance, hear the noisy approach of man and usually slink out of his way. Not so friend bear; *he* stays where he is until well-nigh trodden on, then jumps up in an access of fright and slashes wildly with his paws before fleeing. I was to see several cases of men who had been fearfully mutilated in this manner before I finally left Siam.

I hadn't been long in the Mae Lah basin before I began to grow seriously alarmed about the bear menace. The little F.D. girdling party, who had not yet finished all the girdling and who were camped a mile or two away from me, was pursued by one of the brutes one morning, and the members only saved their skins by swarming up some bamboo. And from them I learnt that if you're chased by a bear you must always run downhill and never up, the reason being that a bear's hind-legs are longer than his fore-legs, and that in consequence he is at a disadvantage when going down a slope. As for climbing anything, a tree is out of the question, for a bear will be up it ten times quicker than you, but bamboo stems, being thin and smooth and slippery, afford his claws no grip.

Shortly after the girdling party incident I achieved the distinction actually of treading on a bear, thus becoming, I should imagine, the only man who has done this and lived on undamaged. I was scrambling over some dead bamboo stems that had drooped right down to earth and formed a sort of crazy lattice-work over it, when the stems suddenly heaved up under my feet and I was thrown on to my back. On struggling upright again I perceived that a bear, terrorised by my unexpected weight on top of it, was dashing away through the network of bamboo and that my coolies, who were ahead of me and directly in its course, were running for their lives to right and left. Luckily the bear kept straight ahead and disappeared from sight without mauling anyone, but the incident brought the danger unpleasantly home to me, and I thought that we'd be fortunate if we emerged from the Mae Lah basin as whole-skinned as we went into it. I could do nothing, however, to minimise the risk; I had no rifle, and even if I'd possessed one I couldn't carry it about with me continually.

There were the wild elephants, too, up in the hilly sources of the Mae Lah. I never actually saw them, but often followed the paths they made while going to and from work, and I hoped my two baggage elephants wouldn't wind them and " desert." Orwell had lost several animals, he had told me, through their getting rid of their hobbles and then joining up with their wild brethren.

It was while this subject was occupying my thoughts that a native chief from Nakon appeared on the scene, and set his men about building an elephant trap directly below my camp. At a point where the Mae Lah had very steep and unscalable banks, a row of bamboo stakes, with a drop-gate in the middle, was run across the stream. Another row, further down round a bend in the river, but without exit of any kind, was then erected, and the trap, so simply effective, was complete: All that remained was for the chief to round up the elephants in the sources and then drive them down the bed of the stream and in through the top end of the trap, and I, whose camp was immediately above it, made frantic preparations to evacuate; to have a few dozen flustered wild elephants charging through the tent being not to my

ELEPHANT "STRAIGHTENING OUT."

liking. Suddenly, however, and for no apparent reason, the chief dropped the whole affair and returned to the amenities of Nakon, leaving me and the elephants in peace and the trap a mere object of curiosity for the tiger and the panther.

Of course there were snakes, and with them I had three nasty experiences close on top of one another. On the first occasion I was resting after tea in my camp chair with my feet up on a camp stool. Suddenly I heard a slithering noise on the ground-sheet below me and to the left, and, turning my head, beheld the tail end of a cobra disappearing under my chair. The slithering noise then stopped abruptly, which told me that the snake had also stopped— right beneath me!

For a while I sat, frozen as motionless as a statue in the chair. I longed to bolt incontinently, but in order to do so I should have first to take my feet off the stool and place them on the ground, thus exposing them to the danger of being swiftly struck at by the hidden death.

Seconds passed, with neither sound nor movement from either the snake or myself. Then the horrible thought occurred to me that it might be climbing up the back of the chair and that at any moment it might hiss in my ear; at which a great wave of fright seemed to rise up inside me and caused me to perform a feat which I consider to this day a physical impossibility: still in the seated position, and with my legs straight out before me as though they were yet on the stool, I catapulted myself clean out of the chair, over the stool, and out on to the tent verandah, where I landed on my stern. What muscle or muscles

E

supplied the driving power I can't imagine, nor did I pause to ponder thereon; I leapt to my feet and, whirling, saw the cobra emerging from beneath the chair and slithering out by one side of the tent. By the time I had seized a stick only a faint rustle in the fringing jungle told me where it had gone, and I made no attempt to pursue it. An hour or so later I had a most violent attack of indigestion, brought on, I presume, purely by nervous shock.

A fortnight later I had a similar experience, exactly at the same time of day and as I was resting after girdling in exactly the same position. To have two snakes entering one's tent so soon after each other is a remarkable coincidence, and when, later, I told another teak-wallah about it, he said:

" H'm. *I've* been in the country fifteen years without having had a snake in my tent once. *You* get a couple in within six months. *Quite* extraordinary, I call it."

" It is, isn't it? " I remarked innocently.

And it wasn't till four years later, during the whole of which time I never had another snake in my tent, that I realised he thought I was lying like a trooper.

To get back to snake No. 2. I was first aware of it through hearing an unusual rustling in the dead leaves on the ground directly in front of my tent. (In Siam the leaves fall in the cold and hot seasons.) Being still nervy after the first affair, I looked quickly up over the table, which was between me and the outside, to see a real whopper of a snake, much bigger than the cobra, coming at a fast speed over the clearing straight in my direction. I then sprang out of the chair and dashed out round one side of the table just as the snake came in round the other. (I should explain here that the creature had no particular designs on me personally; it was simply on its way from one spot to another and, being half-blind after the manner of its kind, did not sight the tent till right upon it.)

Out in the open I turned round and watched. The snake was going the length of the tent from front to back, but on reaching the back it found itself cornered by the " bathroom," which came right down to the ground. Rearing itself up on its tail, it began feeling all round for an exit, a most weird and revolting spectacle. And as it did so its scaly skin kept scraping against my tin bath with a sound that set my teeth on edge.

I realised almost at once that it was harmless. The chief types of poisonous snakes in Siam are the cobra (plus, of course, the king-cobra or hamadryad), the banded krait, and Russell's viper, and this chap certainly wasn't one of them. He was long, about ten feet, and of a negative dusty-brown colour, which led me to believe he was a rat-snake. Whether he was harmless or not, though, a sudden rage seized me: rage at my tent being defiled by this disgusting, stupid reptile. Inside the tent I saw my stick, leaning against a " hahp "; seizing it, I sprang through to the " bathroom " and commenced swiping about in an endeavour to break the snake's back and thus render it easy to kill.

But it was I who seemed helpless; I belaboured the canvas, the bath, the ground, but try as I might I couldn't get a real hit home; and all the while the horrible, blind, scaly thing was writhing round my feet and legs. I found myself shrieking for my coolies and raining curses at this thing I could not kill and which could not kill me; then rage gave way to fear, the innate fear a man has of any reptile, and I rushed out of the tent, to meet my coolies hastening up with drawn jungle-knives in their hands.

Somehow the snake escaped before they could get in and despatch it, and we heard its swishing rustle going up, up, up the jungle-clad slope of ground behind the camp. It seemed ages before the last sound of it died away, and then I realised I was bathed from head to foot in sweat.

These two incidents left me extremely " snake-conscious." Every rustle in the grass outside my tent, whether by day or by night, set me peering about for some possible intruder, and when I got into bed I felt more than grateful for the protection of the mosquito net, otherwise I should have gone to sleep haunted with the fear of waking up with a cold, scaly form alongside me. But things always went in threes, I told myself (had I not been in no less than three collisions in the same vessel, H.M.S. *Triad*, during the War?), and so I felt certain that sooner or later I'd have another snake adventure.

And I had it. Orwell came out on a trip to see how I was getting along with my work, and as we were inspecting both his and my travelling elephants in the evening, the mahout of the last one to file past us said :

" *Ngu nyai*, master. Big snake." Swinging round on his charge's head, he pointed back up the little path that ribboned out of the clearing. " It hissed at me and my elephant as we passed by it up there."

" A python, I expect," said Orwell laconically to me. " These fellows are always pretty vague. Come on. I'll bring my gun."

We went into his tent. He hadn't brought a rifle out with him, only a shot-gun, and as ordinary shot like Nos. 4, 6 and 8 wouldn't be of much avail against a really large snake, he was beginning to look doubtful when he came across exactly one cartridge of S.G. (buckshot).

" Just the thing," he said, slipping the cartridge into one barrel of his gun. " And now for friend python."

We began walking up the path, the mahout following behind on foot and a mob of curious coolies trailing out behind him. My feelings as we trudged along in the cool evening were mixed; I had by now an unholy dread of snakes, but I had the greatest confidence in Orwell, and if the third incident *had* to occur I'd rather it happened when he was with me.

After we'd gone a few hundred yards the mahout casually informed us we had reached the spot. He then, together with the coolies, retreated across the bed of the Mae Lah to the safety of the other side, leaving Orwell and me on the path by ourselves. Expecting a python, we looked up at the neighbouring trees, but could make out nothing.

" Well," called Orwell after a while to the mahout behind us, " where *is* the snake ? "

" At your feet, master," was the somewhat unexpected reply.

And it was—literally. Glancing down, I saw, just within the scrub that bordered the path, an evil head with a flattened hood behind it, and a long blackish body with grey-white marks on the back tapering away into deeper jungle.

" Steady," said Orwell, his voice dropping to a whisper, " it's not a python. It's a hamadryad."

I hadn't been in the jungle long, nevertheless I had heard all I wanted to about the hamadryad, or king-cobra. Unlike other snakes, which if not asleep glide away on the approach of humans, the hamadryad will not only not give way; it is more than likely it will attack, especially if its eggs are near, and as its speed is said to rival that of a galloping horse over a short space of ground, and as its bite is deadly poisonous, I knew that Orwell and I were in an unenviable position.

" Keep absolutely still," I became aware that my companion was whispering again. " I'm going to shoot."

Slowly—maddeningly slowly, it seemed to me—he raised gun to shoulder. And all the time those un-blinking, deadly-cold eyes were staring at my legs only a few inches away from them. I believe I silently cursed Orwell for his slowness, and I *know* it was only because I feared the snake might be galvan-ised into striking, that I did not turn tail and run; but Orwell was an old hand in the jungle and he realised that a sudden movement on his part might cause the thing to rise and strike in a flash.

At last his gun crashed, whereupon we both cast off all caution and fled for our lives. But we needn't have feared; when we gingerly returned to examine the body we found that the horror's head had been blown clean off by the buckshot, though even then we made it thirteen feet six inches long by the tape-measure I used when checking up on the girths of teak trees. Complete with head it must have gone to over fourteen feet, and as fifteen is the outsize limit for a hamadryad, Orwell had shot a pretty specimen. I had it skinned like the leopard-cat, then " mounted " the skin on the branch of a tree, and it looked quite life-like. So much so that if an unsuspecting villager passed my camp and saw it, he nearly jumped out of *his* skin. Indeed, the amusement both I and the coolies got out of scaring innocent passers-by lasted us for weeks.

I was to see plenty more snakes during my jungle roamings in Siam, but never, I am thankful to say, did I repeat such nerve-racking experiences with them. For snakes are—horror!

## CHAPTER SIX

## VALLEY NIGHTS AND DAYS

IT was during one of Orwell's visits to the Mae Lah that I pointed out to him a swelling which had developed on the shoulder of one of my baggage elephants. As I was camped in one spot over a long period of time, she and her companion naturally were waxing fat in idleness; nevertheless, I might have to shift camp suddenly, and with a howdah pressing on the swelling, Mae Foom (that was the patient's name) would suffer considerable pain. Orwell caused her to kneel so that he could inspect the place closely, then turned to me:

" It's a boil," he said briefly. " And wants lancing. Got a pen-knife? "

I produced one, handed it him, then hastily retreated to a safe distance. What, I wondered, happened when one pierced an elephant's boil with a pen-knife?

To my astonishment, nothing very hair-raising occurred. Though Orwell drove the point well home, Mae Foom merely rolled her vast body a little and gurgled through her trunk.

" Now," went on Orwell calmly, " I'll give you an elephant syringe, and I want you to work at the boil every evening with your fingers and then spray it with permanganate of potash."

The syringe was a foot long, rather like the type

you squirt roses with at home, and the following evening, armed with that and a bucket of warm water
tinged a purply-red with p.p., I weighed in. It was
a filthy job, kneading the boil, which was the size of a
football, with one's bare hands, but the rumble of
satisfaction from poor old Mae Foom as the warm,
cleansing water from the syringe went in made everything worth while, and it wasn't long before the place
healed up altogether.

While treating her I met Poo Kam Sen, probably the
finest tusker Siam has ever produced, for he stood well
over nine feet at the shoulder (try and visualise him as
nearly double that height if he stood on his hind-legs,
and then you'll get some idea of his immensity), and
in all respects was physically the perfect elephant.
He belonged to a native chief who had chosen the
Mae Lah as affording good grazing grounds, and
little did I think as I gazed in awe at him that in a few
months' time he would run amok and terrorise the
whole of our Muang Ngow forest, and that Orwell,
who was the bravest of men, would fight an epic
duel with him. But of that more in a later chapter.

When the cold weather was at its height, in January,
the jungle was perfect, rather like an English wood in
spring, with plenty of shade in spite of the falling
leaves, a brilliant blue sky above, and a freshness in
the air that never allowed the shade temperature to
mount above 82° at 2 p.m., the hottest part of the day.
Directly the sun went down the temperature fell with
astonishing rapidity, and I had a huge log fire, the
size of a bonfire, made up outside my tent. After
dinner I would sit out by it, watching the sparks
cascading into the darkened, wind-foaming jungle,

and listening to the kettle which was to make my toddy singing in the hot wood-ash. Happy? I doubt whether man in his estate could have attained to a greater happiness than mine in those peaceful hours. It is the fashion nowadays to sneer at the " wide, open spaces "; indeed, the phrase is so hackneyed that one hardly dares use it. But it is only those who have never known the wilds who do the sneering, I notice.

The nights in bed, though, were far from comfortable; by dawn the thermometer had fallen into the forties, a drop of some forty degrees from the hottest part of the day, with the result that, however many blankets I piled on to me, I still shivered. And it was only through the tip of a missionary whom I met later that I overcame the cold by placing sheets of old newspaper underneath the thin camp mattress. As he said :

" It's no use piling mountains of things on top of you when you've next to nothing *underneath* you. You'll find newspaper a good non-conductor."

Gradually the days grew warmer and the nights less chilly as the cold weather merged into the hot. The leaves were nearly all off the trees by now, and they crackled frostily as one walked over them. Jungle fires became frequent, and, though not as dangerous to life as Canadian forest fires, they charred the vegetation for miles around, and set great teak trees burning like torches. I usually returned from my work as black as a sweep, but this was very slight discomfort compared to what one suffered during the rains, while the heat itself, so far from being enervating, gave one a marvellous feeling of bodily well-being.

There is a strange, inexplicable beauty in very dry, burnt-up forest. The parched, yellow ground is so *clean*, and the thousands of quiet trees, stretching bare arms to the brassy skies as if imploring rain, resemble the pillars of some vast, open-air cathedral. Although cicalas are shrilling in millions, there is a tremendous sense of peace about, a peace that is heightened at the setting of the sun. Then it is as though one were alone with the Almighty at the farthest rim of the world.

I made a habit periodically of visiting the camp of the F.D. girdling party in order to lodge any slight complaints. The ranger in charge of the work was an extremely pleasant, educated Burman, but, alas! on my going to the camp one smoking hot evening I learnt that he had just been carried off up the Nakon road suffering from blackwater fever. At which I remembered the old-timer in the s.s. *Blank*, and reflected that most of his stories had probably been true.

The Nakon road, which ran actually across the Mae Lah river not far from my camp, was dried of all its mud by the middle of the hot weather, and I was able to indulge in some practice rides on Sunstar of an evening. I soon reached the stage of being able to say I could ride, but I never progressed very much further; to become a real horseman you *must* learn young.

These outings in the cool of the evening on Sunstar were lovely. Up and down swelled the undulating road, with the calm, yellow forest stretching for mile upon mile on either side. The wind caused by Sunstar's pace, and he was one of the fastest ponies in the north, soughed through my topee with a sound reminiscent of telegraph poles thrumming in a gale at home, and tingled my face with its hot, dry touch. Every now and then some creature of the wild would flash across the road in front of Sunstar's head: a red, foxy-looking wild dog, a gorgeously-coloured jungle-cock, a red squirrel, a barking-deer. And once I saw a most extraordinary animal. It had the snout of a bear and was about the size of a bear, but since its body ended in a long, bushy tail it looked something like a cross between a hyena and a South American ant-eater, if such can be imagined. I saw it twice, first momentarily, then in plain view quite close to me for a good half-minute, and it could not have been any of the better-known animals. If anyone who reads these lines could give me some idea as to its identity, I should be grateful.

Now that the jungle was burnt out I became much more aware of bird-life than before. There was a beautiful white bird, of the size of a sea-gull only much more graceful, that flitted up and down the bed of the Mae Lah and reminded me of the soul of some beautiful woman, I don't know why. He was the only one of his kind I saw, and was very different from the common white plover that also haunted the river. Another species of plover, black and white but uncrested, swarmed in hordes all over the jungle, and they were about the noisiest creatures imagin-able; at the slightest excuse—a rustle in the under-growth, the scamper of some gibbon in the tree-tops— they would rise in clouds, shrieking " did-you-do-it? " " did-you-do-it? " to one another till you wanted to yell back at them to stop.

I saw two species of kingfisher: one all blue and gold, the other a little spotted grey creature whom the uninitiated might mistake for a snipe. The grey one was the most energetic of the two, for he twittered and hovered over the still river pools in search of tiny fish from earliest dawn till nightfall.

The giant hornbill was fairly common, and I often heard his huge wings swishing through the air, and his raucous " kok-kok-kok " as he alighted on some branch. It is his habit to wall his mate into a tree at nesting time, a slight aperture only being left through which he can feed her, the idea being, I suppose, to ensure she gets on with her job of hatching the eggs. The same custom, I have heard, applies to the Australian love-bird. Hornbills cannot be recommended as pets, as they are very verminous.

Green parrakeets and minas were common. They both make good pets, minas especially being first-class imitators and therefore good talkers. Doves and green pigeons were also numerous, the latter having a lovely soft green plumage and bright blue or bright red claws. They invariably perched on the top of the very highest trees, and their presence could only be detected by the clear, pure whistles they uttered from time to time. Jungle-fowl, the originators of the domestic variety, though I rarely saw them on the wing, could be heard crowing and scuttling in the brakes all round my camp, and I longed for the gun I was to possess later. The breast feathers of the male, incidentally, are much sought after by trout fishers.

There were no duck or teal or snipe in the vicinity, as these flourished in the flatter, more marshy districts

further to the south. I was soon to come across
them, however, as, when the next monsoon season
was shrouding the jungle in rain, I received instructions to proceed to the company's No. 1 Rafting Station
at Sawankaloke, a place situated on the main Mae
Yome river well below the hilly teak forest area. I
was to relieve a married man who wished to return to
Bangkok, apparently, and as I should be away from
the jungle proper for some months, I sold Sunstar to
a missionary in Nakon, after first pointing out the
occasions on which he became the Yellow Peril.

I then boarded the first train I had seen or heard for
some considerable time.

## CHAPTER SEVEN

# I GO DOWN RAFTING

" RAFTING " was a job at which the teak-men were apt to turn up their noses. It was beneath them, they vaguely hinted, and fit only for white-faced office-wallahs from Bangkok. Personally, I found the job one of great responsibility, carried out under appalling conditions, and without the romance of the jungle on the one side or the amenities of civilised Bangkok on the other.

The idea of rafting is that obviously you cannot allow thousands of logs to come drifting out of the jungle rivers and then down the great main river Mae Nam into the populated water-way of Bangkok; somewhere the logs have got to be caught and collected into rafts which, manned by river experts, can be brought down under control to the capital. But rafts cannot negotiate waterfalls, and the companies therefore built their stations immediately below the southernmost falls of the various main rivers. Generally speaking, the stations were about 200 miles south of the forests and 300 miles north of Bangkok; they were thus in a sort of no-man's-land, neither up-country nor down.

As stated, I was detailed to Rafting Station No. 1, which was on the Mae Yome at Sawankaloke. I got there by taking, first the main-line train, then a branch one which deposited me at Wang Mai Korn, a filthy little native town perched on stilts on the left bank of the Mae Yome. I then went by boat a few miles up-stream and arrived at Sawankaloke, which consisted, I found, of a temple, a straggling but quite clean village, and the rafting stations of three teak companies.

My own firm's station was composed of an extremely nice bungalow with an office beneath, a large godown containing rattan and other stores, and a few odd outhouses, the whole being surrounded by a well-kept compound in which beds of bright flowers smiled a welcome to the new-comer. Immediately in front of and below the compound ran the Mae Yome, whose banks here were a good thirty feet high.

A very big rise had occurred, I learnt from Richmond, the man whom I had come to relieve, a fortnight ago, bringing thousands of logs down from the north. These logs had been caught and brought into the banks by the villagers for the usual salvage money paid them by the firms, and now the licensed raftsmen—swarthy Siamese, for we were now south of Lao territory—were engaged in making the timber up into rafts containing an average of 160 logs apiece. Our job, Richmond told me, was to supervise the work in general, settle disputes between rival raftsmen, advance them money, take all rafts measurements when the rafts were completed, and then send them off on the first stage of their long journey down to Bangkok.

After a period in Sawankaloke, the four of us, Richmond, his wife, myself and a small dog the size of a lozenge, which suffered abominably from ticks, moved forty-five miles down-stream to a place called Sukothai, where the company's second rafting station

THE ELEPHANT THAT WOULDN'T.

was situated. We went in the only launch the river boasted of, which launch seemed liable to disintegrate at any moment. Between Sawankaloke and Sukothai the river was not only very fast and very narrow, but it bristled with snags of every kind and description; at one bend a shoal would suddenly be encountered; at another a huge clump of fallen bamboo the size of a house would loom up ahead and threaten to catch us in its toils; at yet another a stump under water would nearly tear the bottom out of the launch; but somehow we got through and arrived unscathed at our destination.

At R.S. No. 2 the logs that had escaped being salved up-stream at Sawankaloke were being made up into rafts by the natives of Sukothai, and at Sukothai I was to remain until both lots of rafts had passed right through to the south on their way to our third rafting station at Paknampoh. After another week of showing me the ropes, Richmond and his wife and the lozenge-like dog departed up-stream in the launch, bound for the distant town of Wang Mai Korn, where the branch railway began. As they rounded a bend they turned and waved happily to me, relief written all over their faces (I include the dog's) at the prospect of a speedy return to Bangkok.

I didn't wonder then at their behaviour, and I don't now. For of all the desolate, miserable, God-forsaken places on this earth, Sukothai must surely be the worst!! Was it fit for a white woman? It wasn't fit for a white man. It wasn't fit for a Lao or a Kamoo; the servants I'd brought down with me told me so! It was the theatrical idea of the West Coast of Africa in the old days come to life again.

F

To begin with, the banks of the Mae Yome, instead of being thirty feet high like they were at Sawan-kaloke, were only about seven feet above the river-bed, with the result that in the rains the whole district was in a perpetual state of semi-flood. The country all round consisted neither of the green, jungle-clad hills of the north nor of the fertile paddyland of the south; it was just one vast, flat, desolate swamp of mud, cane and elephant-grass. The only other white men in Sukothai—or indeed anywhere for a hundred miles in any given direction—were two Danes and an Englishman, all rafting assistants for their respective firms like myself. Of these, one Dane eventually resigned and went home to Denmark, the second was invalided because he imagined everyone was trying to poison his drink, and the Englishman I last saw endeavouring to sell tinned meat in the Wandsworth Road, London. I don't wonder they all left Sukothai.

The heat there was appalling, far worse than in the jungle proper. Though the rains were on, the sun managed to glare through the aching white of the clouds and, catching the yellow waters of the river, reflect itself back again, thus making a sort of double glare. The firm's compound was a dismal affair, small and viewless and heat-containing—it couldn't have been anything else under the circumstances—the town strung along the banks was dirty and de-pressing, while the Siamese inhabitants were sombre and surly-looking, in striking contrast to their usual smiling selves; it was as if they knew they lived in a place thoroughly to be ashamed of.

The river-water, which had to serve for both wash-ing and drinking purposes (drains, wells, taps and pipes being, of course, non-existent), was so dirty that I subjected it to three stages of purification before I dared drink it; first I placed alum in it to cause the worst of the dirt to sink to the bottom of the bucket in which it had been drawn, then I filtered it, and then I had it boiled. Even then a few germs must have been left, for two days after the Richmonds departed I had a severe attack of colic. I had suffered recently up in the Mae Lah from a certain amount of digestive troubles, but had put them down to the normal effects of the climate; as in England, for instance, colds and kindred ailments are the danger in the winter, so out East do you have to guard against stomach disorders, especially in the cold and hot seasons. This colic go, however, was most unpleasant, and left me feeling pretty shaky.

The work at Sukothai was very hard, but it was all the more welcome in that it helped one to forget about Sukothai. " Fleas are good for a dog; they keep a dog from brooding on being a dog." By day one spent most of the time out on the aching shine of the river, skipping from raft to raft, measuring, recording, and every now and then yelling to some raftsman who was threatening a jam. There were hundreds of rafts wanting a mooring-place, and it was a miracle that the river at Sukothai didn't get so hopelessly blocked that timber could never move again; the two Danes, the other Englishman and myself, our interests being identical, worked in unison as far as possible, and as I was newer to the country than they I must have given some comical orders. The word " pare " means " goat " or " raft " according to the tone, and I must often have shouted to some swarthy Siamese telling him to tie up his " goat " at once to the bank.

At night one worked on accounts and a multitude of other clerical matters in the tiny office in the company's little bungalow. With an oil-lamp, suspended from the ceiling, shedding a little light and a great deal of heat over the already suffocating compartment, with moths and bugs buzzing and bumping from roof to desk, with the whine of millions of mosquitoes (Sukothai's only contented inhabitants) making a continuous background of sound in the ears, with itching bumps on the hands and sweat pouring down the pallid brow, one grappled with figures till far into the sweltering night in truly " the white man's grave " style. And when that attack of colic doubled me up at the desk into the bargain, the simile became realistically apparent. Eventually one went to bed in a room where the heat seemed even worse, to lie tossing and turning while the hot rain tumbled on the roof and the owls, of which there were many, hooted to one another outside.

The only time I witnessed anything remotely pleasurable in Sukothai was when the people held their boat-races. There were no classes—eights, fours and so on; boats of all sizes could join in any particular race, and they did. From the tiniest dug-out manned by one paddler to huge, barge-like craft simply packed with men, women and children, they lined up across the river, then at the word of no one in particular, as far as I could see, off they started. The speed developed was astonishing, but there was no winning-post, nor did it apparently matter who won; the boats simply went on and on till, overloaded as they were, they filled up and capsized, leaving multitudes of dark heads bobbing up and down on the yellow river waves. No one drowned, for both old and young could swim like corks.

At last came the time when the experts in the shape of the firm's native clerks and senior raftsmen adjudged the river to be just right for despatching the rafts on down to Rafting Station No. 3 at Paknampoh. We four whites then held a conference, and agreed.

The decision was a nice one. If the river was still a little too high, or if there was a likelihood of a further rise occurring, then the rafts would run the risk of being broken up or washed over the banks of the Mae Yome lower down; on the other hand, were they to be kept too long at Sukothai, the river might have fallen so low by the time they were half-way to Paknampoh that they would strand on sand-bars and remain there till the following rains. If the worst occurred either way we, as rafting assistants, would naturally get the blame, since we were responsible, and it was therefore with some anxiety that we gave the order which once issued could not be cancelled.

Before starting, each raftsman launched a tiny bamboo craft in which were placed offerings of candles and fruit and flowers for the propitiation of the all-powerful river-god, the firms allowing a special grant of two *ticals* for this purpose; then one by one, as we directed, the long, snake-like rafts started off on their 140-mile journey to R.S. No. 3 at Paknampoh.

The construction of the rafts, which were put together with a skill that only many years' experience could perfect, deserves a word. They were about ninety yards long, and consisted of about 160 logs arranged in sections of ten one behind the other, each section averaging sixteen logs tied abreast with cane. The sections in the middle were the broadest, being about fifteen yards across, while those at the bow and stern were much narrower, with the result that the rafts, if viewed from above, had the appearance of huge skeleton punts.

In the foremost bow section were two sweeps whose purpose was to propel the head of the raft round difficult bends in the river. Amidships were several logs on each side which were allowed to swing free, the logs thus acting as fenders to the parent body. On the stern section was a wooden bollard round which was coiled the stout hempen rope required for securing the raft at night.

The work of securing was done as follows. The raftsman in charge had four coolies under him: two at the sweeps, one for miscellaneous work, and one for mooring at night or in any emergency. The latter coolie was armed with a long pole, one end of which was spiked and the other tied to the free end of the length of rope round the bollard. At a word from the raftsman this man would swim ashore with the pole and, after clambering up the bank, dig the spiked end into the earth. Grasping the top end with both hands, with his feet braced against the ground and the whole weight of his body straining backwards, he would hang on in this fashion while the raftsman on board eased the rope round the bollard and gradually reduced the way of the raft till it was stopped altogether. To moor the stern and bow to trees on the bank was then a simple matter.

For living quarters the men built a little attap-roofed shelter near the stern, and they took enough food with them to last them from one rafting station to the next, villages on these river stretches being practically non-existent. Taking them as a whole, the raftsmen were a fine, strong, efficient crowd with whom it was a pleasure to deal; only occasionally was a bad hat encountered, and then unfortunately he *was* a villain.

When the last of the rafts had left Sukothai, I myself thankfully departed from the place in order to see the timber through the royalty stations at Paknampoh. I went by the crazy launch up to Wang Mai Korn, thence by branch- and main-line trains down to Paknampoh. I thus completed in two days a journey that would take the rafts a fortnight, and arrived at my destination a good forty-eight hours before the very first of the rafts to leave Sukothai appeared on the scene.

On the next page I give a rough map, not to scale, illustrating the whole of the ground covered by the logs from the Muang Ngow forest in the north to the last raft-ing station above Bangkok at Paknampoh (R.S. No. 3), and showing the various rivers, roads and railway lines we used to travel along in connection with the work.

At Paknampoh I put on airs, for the place boasted, not only of a railway station, but of a cinema. I invested in a collar-stud and a bow-tie, and in com-pany with the two Danes, who, like me, had come down by train from Sukothai in order to catch up with their rafts, we went one evening to the cinema, where in an atmosphere that would have cooked an egg we watched the antics of Charlie Chaplin and

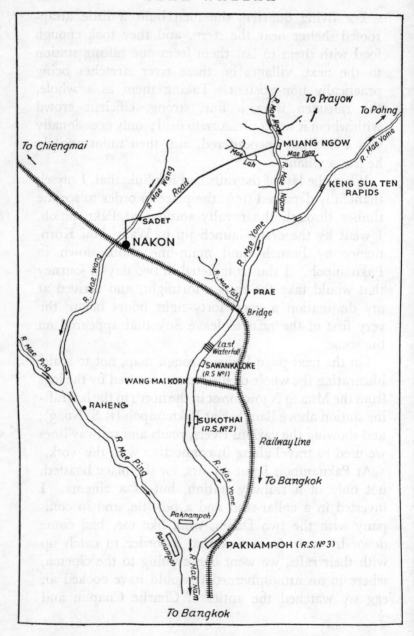

wondered why he didn't burst into flames. We then repaired to the Danes' bungalow and fed gigantically on tinned Danish food—pâté de foie gras, sweet gherkins, tongue, black pudding in syrup being but a few of the dishes. We also drank in Ny Carlsberg beer the health of the Englishman who was still languishing in Sukothai.

They were good fellows, those Danes: the very best. They spoke both English and Siamese fluently, they were of magnificent physique, and there was nothing they wouldn't do for you. I believe the one who was eventually invalided home soon recovered from his neurasthenia, and if either he or his friend should read these lines I give them " Skold! "

The duties at Paknampoh were much lighter than at either of the other two rafting stations, and there were first-class launches available to take one up and down the river. It was here the great rivers Mae Yome (to avoid confusion I omit all mention of the teakless Mae Narn) and Mae Ping joined together to form the huge Mae Nam, or Mother of Waters, that flowed on in unbroken majesty for another two hundred miles before reaching Bangkok and the sea. Our firm's compound was on the left bank of the Mae Yome immediately above the confluence, and the busiest part of the town proper was strung along the right bank of the main Mae Nam just below it.

A few hundred yards up the Mae Ping were the compounds of two British firms which worked both their own teak and a little of ours down the Mae Ping and its tributary the Mae Wang. I and the Danes found the representatives of these firms present, and with five of us whites all within a mile of one another we seemed quite a crowd. We took it in turns to act the host, and had some convivial evenings together in which not one single game of bridge was played. But perhaps that was because there were five of us.

Neither, for the information of certain playgoers and readers of fiction, did we reel about in filthy, tattered " whites," hiccuping violently and every now and then throwing a couple of coolies over an adjoining godown just for fun.

Neither did we go in for *drugs*.

Neither had any of us come out from home to *forget*.

The rains ceased and the cold weather, a far less virile cold weather than the one I had experienced in the teak forests of the north, began. The last of the rafts got safely through and off to Bangkok, and then I was detailed to return up-country on a " neaping " expedition.

## CHAPTER EIGHT

## SOME RIVER JOURNEYS

EVERY year so many logs floated out of the Mae Ngow river into the Mae Yome. Every year a large proportion of these arrived on the big rises in the rains at R.S. No. 1 at Sawankaloke. The remainder, therefore, were left lying stranded somewhere along the stretch of the Mae Yome between the mouth of the Mae Ngow and the waterfall just above Sawankaloke. To check up on this (and the numbers never *did* quite tally, for a good many logs became permanently lost in overgrown side-creeks of the Mae Yome), to make a note of the general progress of the timber, to report on big stacks necessitating elephant clearance, and to take steps against such stacks catching fire through the carelessness of passing fishermen, I was to travel by boat from Sawankaloke up the Mae Yome to the mouth of the Mae Ngow. This job, which is done every year on all the teak-carrying rivers of the north, is called " neaping." " Stock-taking " would be just as applicable a term.

Back I went by train from Paknampoh to Wang Mai Korn. In order to stretch my legs after the journey, I decided to dispense with the hired boat that was waiting to take me the four miles between Wang Mai Korn and our rafting compound at Sawankaloke, and to walk up the cart-road that ran along the bank. This road, I had heard on my previous visit, bore an evil reputation; dacoits and thugs were apt, I was told, to leap out of the fringing jungle and strangle the innocent passer-by, and Swan, our man at Pohng to whom I had delivered the specie, had himself told me that once he had been attacked while carrying a bag of money along this particular strip of road. However, I comforted myself by the fact that I had nothing valuable on me, and started off.

As I trudged along, with the now sunken Mae Yome river below me to the right and the jungle immediately on my left, Swan and his story kept turning over in my head.

Swan was one of the most remarkable men one could meet, for, amongst other characteristics, he possessed a charmed life; without any exaggeration, nothing and no one could hurt him. He survived the killings of the terrible man-eating tigress of Pohng, of which more in a later chapter, he was always falling off his horse on lonely jungle paths yet never coming to harm, and during my own brief stay in his bungalow he had (a) singed most of his hair off through inspecting a dead beetle too close to the naked light of a lamp, and (b) fallen backwards over the verandah railings on to the compound below. It was a goodish drop, and amply sufficient to break the neck of any ordinary man, but Swan had merely picked himself up and, climbing back by the steps, resumed the conversation where it had been interrupted.

The story he told me was that, having been detailed off for rafting one year, he was walking up to Sawankaloke with a large bag of money in his hand, when a native had stolen up behind him and clouted him over the head with some heavy weapon.

" Over I went," continued Swan, " flat on the ground. The bag fell out of my hand, and by the time I got to my feet again the fellow was just disappearing into the jungle with it. So I started after him . . ."

" But weren't you hurt? " I had broken in.

He dismissed such an absurd question with a brief shake of the head: " Hadn't made more than a few yards through the jungle when I noticed that the bag must have got torn in the excitement, for the thief was leaving a trail of *ticals* behind him, like in a paper chase. Result was that I didn't know whether to go on and catch him or to stop and pick up the *ticals* as I went along." Here Swan had stopped to laugh at the memory.

" Well? " I prompted, " what happened in the end? "

" In the end we neither of us got the money. The thief went on running till there wasn't a piece left in the bag, and I got lost."

On finishing the story Swan had laughed harder than ever, and I had joined in. Now, however, that I was in the same locality, the joke had lost its savour and I felt decidedly ill at ease. For the road *was* lonely, unutterably lonely. I had spent hundreds of hours, travelled hundreds of miles on equally deserted jungle paths up north, but here it was somehow different; this strip of roadway, fringed by the green and quiet jungle, seemed to breathe out a cold, deadly terror.

And then, as I was trying to laugh away my fears,

on rounding a bend I came full upon the body of a murdered man.

He was lying across the road upon his face, his arms spread-eagled, and the back of his head bashed in. Approaching gingerly, I bent over him; the injury was fairly fresh, not more than two or three hours old, if that, I reckoned, and had evidently been caused by someone creeping up behind him and hitting him with some heavy weapon. Swan's luck had held; this poor Siamese's hadn't.

I stood by the corpse. Only the faint, indefinable murmur of the river broke the eerie silence, and it occurred to me that at this moment the murderer might be crouching, malignant and furtive, behind the wall of green. I regretted that I had not brought my pistol with me.

Suddenly I heard the sound of bare feet whispering on the road; the feet were still invisible, as there was another bend immediately above where I stood, and I waited to see who would appear.

The murderer appeared—chained to two bare-footed, khaki-clad gendarmes who walked on either side of him. He was a Siamese of about twenty-five, sullen of face and with very short cropped hair. Without a word to me or even a glance in my direction, the three passed by me and vanished down river, and I was again alone with the corpse.

This last happening—the sudden appearance and disappearance of the murderer—was weird in the extreme, and left one with the feeling that everything was taking place in a dream. For a while I remained with the body, being strangely reluctant to leave the pitiful thing to the ghostly loneliness of the road, then at last I tore myself away and resumed my journey up to Sawankaloke.

On arrival at our rafting compound I found that the news had spread around in the uncanny way it does in any wild country.

" The man who die, he a bad man," explained the Siamese clerk in charge of our station. " He go after another man's wife, and the husband, he get mad. He wait this morning in the jungle, then jump out and kill—so."

" How dost thou know all this? " I naturally asked.

" Master, I know," was all I was vouchsafed.

" The body," I said. " Why hasn't that been removed? "

" It wait for the Nai Umphur to come and inspect it." The clerk paused, and chewed betel-nut reflectively. " I think master take care he not go down that road any more by himself. I think he go either by boat or with two of the compound coolies in future. That road, it a bad road."

I heartily agreed.

That evening, while the clerk was arranging about the boats which were to take me on the morrow up the Mae Yome for the " neap," I went over to see my Danish friends, who had left Paknampoh before me and who were now, I knew, in Sawankaloke. The three of us had tea on the shady verandah overlooking the compound lawns, and mighty peaceful and enjoyable the whole scene was. My friends' dogs were chasing one another across the compound in play, and as I idly watched them I became aware that I had been sadly missing something for a year and more.

"I'd give anything for a dog," I murmured.

"A dog?" The taller of the Danes spoke in his deep voice. "You shall have one. Hey, Sclave!"

"Sclave" came up the verandah steps in obedience to the call, and he was the queerest little dog ever man saw, being a sort of cross between an English fox-terrier and a bull-terrier, with a dash of dachshund thrown in, if you can imagine such a creature. His short coat was black and white, and to add to his comicality both tail and ears had been clipped short.

"What's 'Sclave' mean?" I asked.

"A slave. A coward you would call him in English."

I stretched out my hand and called to "Sclave." He approached and sniffed, and in that one second the bond between us was complete. My heart went right out to this queer little chap, while in me he seemed to recognise the master he had always longed for. When I rose to return to my own compound he followed me without my having to call him, and that night he slept on the floor beside my bed. For me it was like the start of a new phase in one's life.

Next day we went off neaping. I had two boats: a very small dug-out, paddled or poled by two Lao boatmen, for my own personal use, and another much bigger affair with a bamboo cover for my tents, baggage and servants.

I found neaping almost as blissful as travelling along the Nakon–Muang Ngow road. Every day that passed saw our little party further up into the familiar jungle hills, and every night we put up our tents on

JUNGLE PEACE.  JUNCTION OF MAE NGOW AND MAE YOME RIVERS.

some new sand-bank giving some new view of the river. The work was light, consisting as it did of noting the numbers and classifications of the stranded logs as we passed them, and of clearing brushwood and other debris away from stacks to lessen the chances of fire. Very often we would strike four-mile stretches of log-free river, when there would be nothing for me to do but to watch the green banks sliding by and occasionally help the boatmen haul the dug-out up the numerous little rapids. Peace? There can be nothing more peaceful and soothing to the mind than a jungle-fringed river out East in the dry season.

After a week's journey, during which time the only signs of humans other than ourselves were a few tiny villages squatting like beetles on the bank, we came to a railway bridge spanning the river. As we neared it a train thundered by, and I realised with amazement that it was the self-same Pitsanuloke–Nakon train from which eighteen months ago I had peered down on to that foaming river on first going up-country. *Then* I had been the man of civilisation gaping in awe at the wilds. *Now* I was the man of the wilds gaping in equal astonishment at this product of civilisation.

Near the bridge two figures detached themselves from the bank greenery and approached my boats. I recognised them as coolies belonging to the firm's compound in Nakon, and they handed me a note from the Forest Manager. The note instructed me to break off my neap at the bridge, marking the northernmost log included in my count with lime for the benefit of Orwell, who was apparently going to be responsible for the remainder of the count up to

G

the mouth of the Mae Ngow. The F.M. concluded by saying that I was to come into Nakon forthwith, since I was required for the neap of another river.

I received the note without emotion; it seemed, indeed, the most natural thing in the world for it to be delivered to me, yet consider the circumstances. Out of touch with anyone, I had been buried in the wilds for a week, yet my Manager knew almost to an hour when I should arrive at this particular bridge, and had timed the sending-off of his coolies accordingly. Which sort of miracle is brought about by what is known as ORGANISATION.

I marked the northernmost log beneath the bridge with large crosses of lime for Orwell's information, had my boats unloaded, paid off the boatmen, then with the aid of some coolies hired from a neighbouring village carried my kit and tents up the railway embankment and along the line to the nearest station. There was only one train a day for Nakon, and I had just missed that, so I caused a clearing to be hacked in the jungle behind the tiny station, and made camp.

Behold the beautiful simplicity of everything. No yelling porters, no trippers, no time-tables to be consulted, no touts, no backsheesh merchants. You got out of your boats and, pointing to some distant coconut fronds that might denote a village, said to your servants: "Find some carrier coolies." You then sat down and waited, till presently several dusky gentlemen, clad only in loin-cloths, appeared on the scene. To these you said in Lao: "Take kit to railway station, fifty *satangs* each." And they, being unspoilt jungle folk and knowing the price to be fair, made no attempt to argue, but promptly grabbed your kit and took it to the station. As for making camp, such trees as happened to be in your way you just cut down.

When the train arrived the following day, my boy celebrated the event by heaving my suit-case into the carriage by way of the window. There was a terrific crash of splintering glass as the pane went into a thousand pieces, and at the sound the stationmaster, engine-driver and fireman all came hurrying up to see what was the matter.

I could hardly blame the boy, since window-panes were practically unknown in the north and he simply hadn't realised the glass was there. I myself had, on catching a train while rafting, bumped my forehead sorely through leaning out of an open window that wasn't open, so I forebore from scolding him and offered compensation, which was immediately accepted by the courteous, smiling stationmaster. The broken glass was swept up, the driver and fireman (all trains used wood-fuel) resumed their posts, and we were off, Sclave, who by now practically never left my side, lying down at my feet.

On my arrival in the office of our compound at Nakon, the F.M. drew out his map of the north.

"I want you to do the Nakon to Paknampoh neap now," said he.

I glanced at the map, and was well pleased. Down the great Mae Wang river I was to go, out into the mighty Mae Ping, and then right on down this latter river till it met the Mae Yome at Paknampoh. Altogether the journey would be one of about two hundred and fifty miles, through deserted country, and during the three weeks it would take, never once would I be within miles of the railway line (see map on p. 88).

"I've got your boats ready," the F.M. went on. "But first, before you use 'em, I want you to go up to Ban Luang, a village some twelve miles above Nakon on the bank of the Mae Wang, and start counting from there. No need for you to have boats while you're above Nakon, the river's too shallow. Simply camp on the bank, and move your camp down as you go along. A couple of bullock-carts and half a dozen coolies 'll be enough for your kit."

"Right," I said. "When do I start?"

"Better have two days' rest in here first. You can spend 'em in doing your Mae Yome neap figures and in buying a couple of ponies now you're back. Heard about Sunstar and Simmons, by the way?"

Simmons was the missionary to whom I had sold Sunstar, and I shook my head.

"Simmons tried to ride him in the pig-sticking race at Christmas. Of course, soon as Sunstar saw all the other ponies around he was off like a flash. Charged through the rest of the field and out through the gates on down to the market-place, with Simmons on his back still holding the lance for sticking the dummy pig. Best sight round these parts for years. Still, it's lucky Simmons didn't break his neck, and if it hadn't been for Sunstar eventually coming to a standstill of his own accord, I believe he would have done."

"I *know* he would," I muttered. "But I warned him!"

Next day the word went forth that the Nai Misater Khumbeur (which was the nearest approach the

Laos and Siamese could get to my name) desired horseflesh, and once again there filed into the compound turbaned Shans with ponies to sell. They, the ponies, were a better lot than the ones I'd first had to choose from, and presently I selected a red and a black. I then took on a pony-boy and a grasscutter, and my stable was complete.

The day after, two bullock-carts groaned and squeaked into the compound. On them were placed my tents and camp kit, then, followed by my coolies and servants, the carts hit the trail for the village of Ban Luang, twelve miles away to the north.

As I should travel very much faster than they, I remained in the compound, finishing off some clerical work. I had tiffin with the F.M., then about 3 p.m. set out on my new red, with the pony-boy riding behind on the black. At our heels, his tail well up, and utterly disdainful of the mangy yellow pariahs that snarled and slavered at us as we passed through the town, trotted little Sclave.

I had never been in the locality of Ban Luang before, neither had my pony-boy, but the cartmen knew the way and had told me how to follow them up. When we had ridden some eight miles we came to a narrow road on the left of the track we were on; according to information received, this road led straight to the village, so I turned the ponies up it. We had only gone half a mile, however, when it suddenly split into two, leaving me doubtful as to which fork to follow, as the dry, brittle dust on both was plentifully covered with the marks of passing carts. Eventually I chose the right-hand one, and rode on up it a little faster than before.

It grew late. I increased the pace of our ponies, and though Sclave was both short and fat he kept up gallantly. The cold weather was just giving way to the hot, which meant that the nights were very chilly and the days the very opposite. I had become soaked in sweat while riding along the sun-glaring cart-road from Nakon, but now that the air was rapidly cooling off my clothes were beginning to feel unpleasantly clammy.

After we had made another two or three miles without coming to any signs of human habitation, I halted to take stock of our position. We were in flat country, where it is much easier to get lost than in amongst hills, and where the river Mae Wang lay I hadn't an idea. It looked like spending a night in the tall jungle that towered up in grim silence on either side of the little path, and with the temperature dropping every minute I knew this would be no joking matter. No one can do long up-country in Siam without getting infected with malaria, and I had proved no exception to the rule. My bouts so far had been of the mild, " low fever " type, but any exposure to cold on top of being over-heated was almost bound to bring on a severe attack. To add to our discomfiture, neither I nor the pony-boy had, by some extraordinary mischance, brought any matches with us, so it would be impossible to kindle a fire. As for the risks we and the ponies would run from tigers and panthers, they never even entered my head; when a man's in acute physical discomfort he doesn't worry much about danger.

I resolved to push ahead till complete darkness stopped our progress, for the path must lead somewhere. Sclave, however, was very tired by now, and to ease him I picked him up before galloping on.

Be with me, riding along a jungle path. On either side is the wall of green, which seems to lean over slightly as though about to fall on you. Sticking out from the green are branches which threaten to sweep you from the saddle, and sharp, cut ends of bamboo (the legacies from elephants with howdahs passing by) that can easily brain you or put out your eyes. Not only have you constantly to duck and twist in the saddle to avoid these dangers, but you've got to watch the path itself, which is full of blind corners and snags in the shape of fallen trees across it, deep depressions and sudden rises. And now, not only was it growing dark, but I had Sclave to hold in one hand while with the other I guided the reins.

As my pony jumped over some obstacle, Sclave was jerked out of my grasp and pitched into a thorn-bush. I reined in, and by the time I had dismounted he was scrambling out, whimpering. The poor little chap was covered in prickles, and there was nothing for it but to start pulling the worst of them off him. And then, while doing this, there came the welcome sound of some Lao singing his high, whining chant to give himself heart in this darkening and lonesome jungle.

We hailed him. Our voices stopped him fear-stricken in his tracks, but my pony-boy managed to shout reassurance to him and he appeared.

" Where is Ban Luang? " I asked. " Is it far? " or " near? " as it might be according to tone.

There was no doubt about the reply. Our new

friend gave a mocking laugh and pointed over the trees :—

"Ban Luang?" he croaked. "*Meh wooi*, a long, long way away."

"And where art thou going?" was my next question.

"I go to my own village, having stayed out in another later than I meant. Wherefore, master, did I sing, being afraid of tigers."

"Then will I go with thee to thy village," I said. "For I and my horses are lost. Lead on."

He took it all philosophically enough, though undoubtedly relieved to have this unexpected company. I suspected him of being a dusky Lothario whom an intrigue with a maiden had caused to stay out unusually late, for it was extremely rare to find a Lao walking by himself in the jungle towards dark. He took the lead, and finally, as the last vestige of light disappeared, we arrived at a tiny village.

"Send me the headman," I said to him, and soon a little man, clad in a pair of dark blue jungle pants and clutching a blanket round his skinny shoulders, appeared. To him I explained my plight, whereupon he promptly conducted me to his own home. In common with other homesteads in Northern Siam, this one consisted of a small yard in which had been erected a one-compartment shanty. The shanty's roof was of dried attap-grass, the floor of split bamboo, and the walls were of plaited cane. To protect it from the dampness of the rains and marauding wild animals, it was raised on stilts about ten feet above the ground, and one reached it by climbing up a rickety ladder.

The good wife, an aged dame with a wrinkled face and kindly eyes, salaamed deeply to me in welcome, then shrilled some orders to her pretty, sloe-eyed daughter, and in less than no time the little family had removed themselves out of the shanty and into a neighbour's, leaving me and Sclave in sole possession. The wife returned shortly with a meal of rice and ducks' eggs and a thin cotton blanket. The blanket was probably the only one the dear old soul possessed, but she lent it me willingly, and after intimating that her palliasse and chock-pillow were also mine to use, again withdrew.

Though I was hungry, my first consideration was to get my cold, sweat-sodden clothes dry, for my teeth were beginning to chatter. My pony-boy had by now got a fire going in the yard beneath the shanty, and, shouting to him, I handed him my breeches, shirt and underclothes. I then wrapped my hostess's blanket round me and shared the food with Sclave. Less than two years ago I had been a naval officer, dressed in naval uniform and entitled to the salutes of all ratings from a chief petty officer downwards. Now I was a shivering creature, wrapped in a buggy blanket and sharing with a dog a messy dish of glutinous rice very different from the rice known to Europeans. Salutes? I'd have been kicked off the quarter-deck of any man-o'-war by the smallest side-boy.

It was after I'd dressed again in dry clothing that I realised how much we in civilisation are dependent on inanimate things such as gramophones and books for taking us out of ourselves. Here, in this compartment lit only by the most primitive of lamps, I had no reading matter, nothing to make me forget myself. So I had a short conversation with my naval friends, in which I told them all about the day's misadventures, then lay down on the palliasse, with my head on the hard bolster, and drew the thin blanket over me.

A minor point of etiquette arose a few moments later through the appearance at the top of the ladder of my host's pariah dog. Every shanty in Siam has its pariah, usually a sunken-flanked, yellow, mangy, flea-bitten creature, and this particular specimen, evidently peeved by the expulsion of its own people and the intrusion of strangers, had climbed up to investigate. Directly he appeared Sclave left my side and was on it like a ton of bricks, with the result that the unfortunate pariah was precipitated head-long down the ladder again, thus receiving injury upon insult.

What was I to do? Was I to blame Sclave, I who had invariably encouraged him to drive mangy trespassers off the premises? How was he to know that I, his all-powerful god, wasn't lord of this home-stead as I was lord of the camps and the bungalows? Yet if the pariah reappeared and I allowed Sclave to heave it down the ladder a second time, it would be giving poor thanks to my host for all his hospitality. Luckily, however, the dog didn't turn up again.

I slept but little that night, being mainly engaged in shivering with cold, so what it would have been like out in the jungle, minus a blanket and roof, and in wet clothes, didn't bear thinking about. I was up soon after dawn, and after saying good-bye to the wife and her pretty daughter, set out in the company of mine ancient host, who was going to guide me to

Ban Luang. I was worried about my cash-box, but on arrival at Ban Luang after two hours' walking found I needn't have feared; the box was safe and sound under the bed in the tent set up ready for me, and the whole camp as ship-shape as though I'd never been absent from it.

As I opened the box with the key I kept on my belt, I did a piece of calculation. A dinner, bed and breakfast at home in England would have cost me about 12s., or six *ticals*. Divide this by half, and I'd still be giving my simple benefactor an (for him) extremely handsome tip. So I handed him three brand-new, crinkly one-*tical* notes, and though he said nothing much, the only emotion a Lao ever really betrays being that of fear, I could see by the way he turned and hurried off home that he was more than satisfied. I then credited myself in my cash account for travelling expenses as follows:

To staying the night at Grand Hotel, Ban Min (the name of the tiny village), and for hire of dragoman . . . . . . . . . . . . . . . . . . . *Tcs.* 3.

And the F.M., who was a great man for humour, duly passed the entry when later he went through my accounts.

Here let me say how, to my certain knowledge, none of the forest assistants ever took advantage of the trust reposed in them by the company in the matter of money. Not only through our immediate travelling expenses, but through the far larger expenses in connection with the handling of a great forest, we could easily have made nice extra incomes for ourselves. We were constantly handing out money for guide work, for compensation for damage done to plantations, etc., by our elephants, for porterage and boat work, for dozens of different types of services, and in ninety-nine instances out of a hundred we were unable to produce vouchers because the simple recipients couldn't read or write. To have slightly " cooked " the accounts by adding a *tical* here and a *tical* there would have been child's play, yet none of us ever did. The company paid us well and didn't boggle over details; wherefore, like Cæsar's wife, were we beyond reproach.

I began my neap, and soon found the Mae Wang a very different river from the Mae Yome. It was much broader, for instance, with the result that now the dry weather was on it consisted mainly of huge sand-banks, with logs scattered here and there over them and a thin ribbon of water meandering in between. In the early mornings this water smoked with the cold, and it was far from pleasant starting off work by wading waist-deep backwards and forwards from one sand-bank to another. By ten o'clock, however, the sand became uncomfortably hot, and by noon I sought the water with relief, for the heat and glare were beyond description. At tiffin-time I climbed the nearest bank and sat in the shade of a tree.

Gradually I worked down the river-bed counting the scattered logs, and when about four miles north of Nakon camped in a handy temple to save the trouble of putting up tents. Rather a lot of timber was in this locality, and on returning to the temple compound on the second evening there after a particularly

long and tiring day in the river, my boy gave me the
welcome news that my cash-box had been stolen.
For some time past now the box had been secured
to my bed, not with the chain required by company
rules, but with a length of rope, as I had lost the chain
in one of my travels and had neglected to get another,
and apparently a robber had rushed into the temple
and cut the rope with a knife.

"And where wert thou at the time?" I asked the
boy.

"I eat the noonday rice in the *sàla* outside," he
answered.

I looked at him suspiciously: "Was the robber
heard?"

"No, master."

"Then how dost thou know he came at noon?"

"The box was there before noon, master, and when
I returned after airing master's bedding, it was
gone."

The answer came pat enough. Doubtful as to
whether he were lying or not, I hastened inside the
temple, accompanied by Sclave, who had been out
all day with me on the river. The box had gone right
enough, and with it had gone my cash for travelling
expenses, amounting to some thirty *ticals*, my automatic pistol, and numerous little personal treasures
in the shape of photographs and gifts from friends.
The pistol could be replaced, and though I should
have to debit myself with the loss of the money as I
had not obeyed company rules, I wasn't worried on
that account. No; it was the loss of those little
treasures, all of which were irreplaceable and yet
of no value whatever to the thief. I turned and,

hastening back across the temple compound, entered the *sala*.

I cross-examined the bullock-cart-men. I cross-examined the coolies. I cross-examined the cook. I cross-examined the boy again, only to find myself at the end in a state of baffled, helpless fury. *Were* they lying, these men who had answered me so glibly and yet so . . . so *dully*? I just couldn't tell. No one, not the greatest detective in the world, could have told. My sensation of helplessness increased.

I began prowling round the village, peering into the faces of the passers-by as though to read their secrets. The news of the loss of the box would by now be all over the place, and in my imagination I felt that everyone was laughing at me. In the cold rage that soon enveloped me I could have burnt that village to the ground!

I summoned the headman, and although I realised the futility of it, asked him if he knew who had stolen the box.

" *Bor hoo, nai*," " Master, I know not," came the inevitable reply, after which there was nothing left but to return empty-handed to the temple.

There, under the shadow of the unwinking Buddha who had witnessed the theft but who would tell me no more than his people, the fit of rage passed, leaving me feeling lonely and—afraid, that was the word. These smiling Laos whom I had thought to be so cheerful and friendly, did not their smiles merely serve as masks to conceal the evil in their hearts? Were not one and all of them robbers and traitors and worse? And was I not in their power for them to do with me as they liked? *They* were the masters, not I.

Sclave approached me, and thrust his soft muzzle into my hands. Whereat the thought struck me that he was every bit as lonely as I, being one little " white " dog amidst a host of yellow pariahs. And so, while the darkness deepened, Sclave and I held hands, so to speak, beneath the altar of Buddha, and told one another how miserable we felt. Hollywood would have given a fortune to have " shot " us then.

My boy approached over the temple compound, a jar of filtered water in one hand, a bottle of whisky in the other : " *Nai cha kin lao whisaky ?* "

Of course I would have my evening tot. As he poured it out after lighting the Hitchcock lamp, I watched him narrowly. He *looked* honest enough, and when I had drunk the whisky I felt better. I had my evening bath out in the temple compound under the gaping stare of the red-mouthed dragons that guarded the walls, and when dinner was over the fit of depression passed completely, and I was able to see matters in their true proportion. Taken as a whole, the Lao, especially the Lao far removed from the larger towns, was a kindly person, gentle and much given to laughter. Only in a few instances did he turn out to be a bad hat, and then, like the little girl in the story, he certainly was horrid. That was the opinion I came to then, and I never had cause to revise it.

The neaping of the Mae Wang where it passed through the town of Nakon proved a nauseating business. The town straggled along both banks, and I had to wade and flounder down the bed between them. A good many of the stranded logs had only very worn and faded hammer-marks on them, so that in order to ascertain which company they belonged to one had to bend right down over them; and it wasn't long before I discovered that the good people of Nakon made of these logs their "conveniences." Added to this, the river itself was fouled by countless elephants, buffaloes and cattle, with the result that by the time I returned to our Nakon compound—I was naturally using it as a base while working through the town—I was in a state that would have caused a Chicago fertilising man to give me elbow room.

After two days I had worked through the town and some way to the south of it, and the time to start my long boat journey arrived. My bullock-carts had already been paid off, and now my boats, the usual small dug-out for myself and the larger one for kit and servants, drew up opposite the company's compound. The F.M. saw me down to the bank.

"Want to see me sneeze?" he queried suddenly.

What does a junior forest assistant say to his boss when asked such a question? Since I *was* his junior, I replied in the affirmative, whereupon he glanced quickly up at the cloudless heavens and then let forth a sternutation that sent the ready plover up in clouds above the trees on the opposite bank.

"I can always sneeze when I look at the sun," he said with satisfaction.

I could well believe him. He was a daring player at polo, and had a great reputation in the north for endurance in the jungle, yet I believe he was prouder of this accomplishment than anything else.

"Well, so long, Campbell."

"So long," I replied, and the boats pushed off. Ahead of me was a lonely journey that would take three weeks, during the whole of which time I would be open to attack from wild animals, dacoits and illnesses. Yet all he had given me was "So long."

And with absolute reason. I stood a great deal more chance of surviving than had I been starting out by car from London to Devonshire, being spared the ghastly risks of an English road.

About forty miles below Nakon the river-bed narrowed considerably, with the result that deepish water stretched from bank to bank. The going now became very pleasant, with no heart-breaking, foot-blistering sand to trudge over. For mile after mile one sat in the dug-out, now watching the tall and graceful trees sliding slowly by on either hand, now leaning forward and grasping the sides of the little craft as it shot with exhilarating speed the numerous little rapids. At times, on rounding a bend, we would surprise a troupe of monkeys drinking at the river's edge, and occasionally great silvery gibbons, some with babes on their backs, could be seen plunging along the leafy air-ways high up overhead.

Once, as I was wading back to my boat after inspecting a log caught up behind some rocks close to the bank, a snake came swimming towards me—a queer sight, like seeing a bit of string swimming. Being waist-deep, I couldn't run out of its way, but it was just as scared of me and sheered off when I splashed, thus narrowly avoiding creating a fourth "incident." Another time a fish, probably a cat-fish, started nibbling my calf as, knee-deep in water, I was bending over a log trying to distinguish the

H

hammer-mark. It goes without saying that I took
steps quickly to remove its meal.

Crocodiles? There were small ones in the river,
but (and altogether I traversed over fifteen hundred
miles of Siam's jungle water-ways in primitive dug-
outs) I never came across a single native who had
ever heard of a man, woman, child or even a dog
being taken by one.

Since sand-banks were few and far between in the
lower Mae Wang, for camping spots we usually chose
one of the little shelves of gravelly sand that in places
sloped down from the bank to the water's edge.
Picture the scene any one of these evenings at the close
of the day's neap. The boats lie alongside the little
shelf, the current gently glucking against their sides.
The river, no longer turbulent as in the rains, murmurs
by, its surface goldened in the sunset. On the further
bank the tall jungle rises, green and cool and quiet.
On the near bank is also jungle, a jungle that looks
darker because it looms closer. The boatmen are
in the act of running up my tent, and my cook is
busy getting tea ready, the smoke of his rapidly
kindled fire rising plume-like in the quiet air. I am
seated on a stool in the middle of the shelf, and Sclave
lies at my side, letting, as only a dog can, the tiny
breeze that every now and then ruffles the river soothe
his eyes and ears. In the dim distances, both up-
stream and down-stream, can be seen the purple
outlines of the everlasting jungle hills. With the
advent of the hot weather even the drone of insects
is hushed, so that the peace of the lulling river is
absolute.

I do not wish to be accused of waxing sentimental,

but those evenings *did* bring such a wonderful peace to the mind, such a sense of utter remoteness from civilisation and all its attendant noise and worries, that one can never forget them so long as one lives.

It was while passing a village about five days' journey below Nakon that I had a first-class view of a buffalo fight. There was very little timber about, and I was idly watching two buffaloes on the bank, when they suddenly took it into their heads to charge one another, and a second later their skulls met with a crack that I can hear to this day.

" Stop," I ordered my paddlers. " Stop and watch."

Nothing loth, the men hove to, and, since the bank was only a few feet above the level of the water and we were only a few feet from the bank, we couldn't have approached nearer to the fight had we wanted to; indeed, I feared at times that the brutes would topple over right on to us.

Once their skulls had met, the buffaloes started circling round and round, head on. This went on for a minute or two, then the forefeet of one slipped and he went down on to his knees, whereupon the other, getting his own head on top, began grinding his adversary's down into a muddy pool that happened to be there.

I thought Buff. No. 1 would be drowned in that tiny pool. He fought and twisted to get free, his neck muscles nearly bursting with the effort; but the muscles of Buff. No. 2 were equally powerful, and for a while his struggles availed him nought. As for myself, I sat lost in wonder that any muscles *could* be so strong as those in the necks of the contending beasts, the sense of power they conveyed to one being stupendous.

Buff. No. 1 was weakening, weakening, weakening. He was going to fall over, be gored to death. . . . My mouth went dry and I was aware that my heart was thrumming.

Buff. No. 1 made a supreme and final effort for life. He heaved sideways and upwards in one awful paroxysm—and got free. A moment later, with such speed that I could scarcely follow it, the tables were turned. In some manner Buff. No. 1 twisted his head round so that, though his horns lay back along the top of his neck, the tip of one entered his opponent's eye. How he could tell that the tip had gone home I didn't know (he couldn't see behind him), but he evidently realised his advantage, for he promptly began goring backwards, thus driving his horn further into the eye socket of Buff. No. 2, a horrible and sickening sight.

A few of the villagers had gathered by now, but they were making no attempt to interfere, whether because they dared not or because they wanted to see more of the fun I could not fathom, and I was thinking that Buff. No. 2 would shortly be giving up the ghost when again a surprising thing happened: No. 1 abruptly relinquished his advantage and turned his back on the other, and, No. 2 being more than content to be out of it, the fight finished as suddenly as it had begun. In spite of the gruelling contest, the only damage that I could see on either was the loss of No. 2's eye, and when finally the owners led them off, one could hardly imagine a fight had ever taken place.

Everyone has heard the story of how the Eastern buffalo can be handled by the tiniest brown child, yet should a white man dare to approach it, he will be charged at once. Well, all I can say is that in the course of my work as a teak-wallah I must have passed through hundreds of buffaloes; I came across them on paddy-fields, on river-banks, in rivers, wherever, in fact, a village happened to be near, and only once did a brute even look like attacking me. They either ignored me or looked at me with the same vacuous stare as the English cow. And it wasn't as if they were accustomed to the presence of white men, the very reverse being the case.

Down in Bangkok many and lurid were the tales one heard of Europeans being chased in Southern Siam, but strangely enough one never came across a case first-hand; it had always happened to a friend of a friend. And the same, I remembered, applied to the stories brought home by naval officers after serving on the China Station. Of course, occasionally white men *are* chased by buffaloes in the same way as they are occasionally chased by cows at home, but on the whole there is no doubt that the average buffalo makes no distinction between humans, brown, yellow or white, and from being constantly put to the plough, it is a good deal less dangerous than the average English bull.

*A propos* of buffaloes, I passed one morning a dead one lying on the bank of the Mae Wang, and its bloated carcass was being torn to pieces by vultures. The scene was loathsome in the extreme, but one couldn't help gazing at it, fascinated. A whole crowd of these filthy birds were pulling at the entrails, flapping their wings and yammering at one another in a sort of high, obscene twitter. New-comers kept soaring down from the heavens, the rush of their sailing pinions sounding most majestical in spite of their disgusting appearance. On alighting they would do a little " run " at the carcass, then plunge into the ghastly feast. Whilst I watched them from the boat a pariah dog suddenly appeared from nowhere, and started jumping and snapping at the vultures in the vain hopes of driving them off and leaving the body to him. What with the increased yammering of the noisome birds, the drooling and twisting of entrails, the yapping of the flea-bitten pariah and the appalling stench that pervaded the air, I was forced to turn my head away with a shudder. I noticed, however, that, far from being disgusted, my two Lao paddlers were positively enjoying the scene; broad grins were on their dusky faces and they were exchanging words about the amusing behaviour of the dog.

" You think that funny? " I asked out of curiosity.

" Very funny, master," they answered, openly and with even bigger grins.

I made no comment but hastened the boat on. That evening there came a marvellous sunset; the sky turned from blue to a medley of colour: pink and flame and crimson and saffron and the most delicate green, while ahead of us the river, catching the glow, resembled a Nan scarf of many hues. Again out of curiosity I glanced at my men. How were they taking it? I wondered.

They weren't taking it. They were ignoring the wonder and the beauty spread out before them.

" See.  The sunset," I said to them.

They twisted their heads round a little towards it.
" Yes," they agreed, " the sun was setting.  Would
master be camping soon? "

" But don't you think it's pretty? " I asked, not to
be driven from the point.

I used the Lao word " ngarm " for pretty, and the
boatmen looked puzzled.  A bracelet was *ngarm*, the
Nakon girls were *ngarm*, but a sunset—they shrugged
their swarthy shoulders and gave me up as hopeless.
Though they were too polite to say so, they evidently
thought it was a pity I didn't know their language
better.  How could a sunset be *ngarm*?  Ludicrous.
The master must have meant something else.

This set me thinking philosophically.  These brown
men had seen humour where I had seen only horror;
yet I had found beauty where they had found nothing
at all.  Who, therefore, had the advantage?  I, the
civilised man, or these jungle Laos?  It seemed to
me we were quits.

And then and there, on that sun-goldened river, I
evolved a theory on life that I call Dead Centre:
which theory has solved everything for me except
the very important matter of how to earn my bread-
and-butter.  And as this is the most important item
for most people, I refrain from explaining Dead
Centre here.

Nine days after leaving Nakon my boats came to
where the Mae Wang river joins the mighty Mae
Ping.  Just above its mouth the Mae Wang narrows
unexpectedly, with high banks on either side which
are crowned with heavy jungle, and it was on this
stretch that we passed a little dug-out, in which sat a

fisherman and his wife with her babe. Neither man nor wife wore clothing above the waist, and their skins were dark with sun. Their faces in the soft evening light wore an expression of wonderful serenity; even the little naked babe at the full breast looked calm and contented, and as I gazed at them I went back hundreds of years, thousands of years. There before me was Palæolithic man, complete with mate and offspring in a dug-out boat, with the dark and primeval jungle overshadowing him and the ageless river beneath. Had I seen nought else on this long journey, that spectacle alone would have made it worth while.

The bed of the Mae Ping river where the Mae Wang ran into it proved to be of colossal width. I estimated it to be at least a mile and a half across, with huge sand-banks that made those I had encountered on the Upper Mae Wang seem tiny in comparison. With this vast amount of river expanse before me, the last and major portion of my neap looked like proving a hot and difficult one, and when a party of Siamese clerks, who had been sent all the way up from Paknampoh to meet me, hove in sight (more organisation, this), I knew I should need their services.

We camped together at the confluence, and it was strange to wake up and see next morning vast expanses of hard, flat sand stretching for miles to north and south, while to east and west all that could be seen of the jungle were thin green filaments against the horizon blue. After breakfast I got my clerks in line, with me in the middle, then in open skirmishing order we started tramping down the bed of the Mae Ping, counting the logs as we came to them. To have done this job alone, zigzagging from one bank to the other, would have taken me months.

It certainly was hot, so hot that by midday even the thick-skinned feet of my clerks and servants could not touch the blistering sand, and, choosing a spot where the shrunken river curved in close to one of the banks, we stopped the boats and climbed up into the welcoming shade of the jungle, there to have tiffin and then rest during the worst heat of the day. I myself wore socks and gym shoes, khaki shirt and shorts, dark goggles and a thick solar topee. In spite of the latter my hair was burnt a tow colour long before we reached Paknampoh, while the rest of me that wasn't covered turned almost black. The heat, intense as it was, proved extraordinarily exhilarating, with the result that at the end of the longest day one merely felt healthily tired instead of exhausted.

The length of the Mae Ping from the mouth of the Mae Wang down to Paknampoh is about one hundred and twenty miles, most of which miles we had to tramp, for in very few places did the river-bed narrow sufficiently for us to get into the boats and rest our legs. We saw but little of animal life, but birds were numerous. Water-crows, a kind of cross between a crow and a duck, repulsive-looking creatures, swarmed, and at evening-time, when they fought and screamed for nesting-places in the trees, the sky was black with them. Snipe and duck were only to be seen in the rains, I gathered from the clerks, but white egrets and comical-looking pelicans (I had never imagined pelicans existing anywhere but in the Zoo) gave interest. We passed two medium-sized Siamese towns, but practically no villages, and my cook had considerable difficulty in supplying me with chickens and reasonably fresh eggs. I got so sick of the monotonous diet that eventually I told him to curry everything he gave me, and it was remarkable what a difference this made; in great heat one never seems to tire of curry.

Twenty-two days after leaving Nakon, and without my having seen a white man, the town of Paknampoh and the huge Mae Nam loomed up ahead. Soon we had come to the mouth of the familiar Mae Yome, and a few strokes of the paddles up this latter river brought the boats to the company's rafting station. In the bungalow I metaphorically washed the sweat of two hundred and twenty miles travel off me, then read the huge mail that the F.M. had redirected from Nakon to await my arrival at Paknampoh. I found the newspapers absorbingly interesting, having been out of the world over three weeks.

The following day I took train back to Nakon. There I handed my neap figures to the F.M., and there I also found Orwell, who had come in from the Muang Ngow forest in order to help in the yearly accounts. And from Orwell I heard the tale of the running amok of Poo Kam Sen.

## CHAPTER NINE

## MAN VERSUS ELEPHANT

BEFORE dealing with the exploits of Poo Kam Sen, I append a few facts concerning the Asiatic elephant.

The Asiatic elephant differs greatly from his African brother. He has shorter, thicker legs, his ears are much smaller, his body is more massive, and he has a great, square head in place of the African's sloping one. The biggest African elephant stands about eleven feet at the shoulder, the biggest Asiatic, ten; ten feet is very exceptional, however, eight being quite a good height for a tusker. The biggest animal I ever saw—Poo Kam Sen—stood nine feet three inches, which is enormous. (Try again to visualise what that would represent were he standing upright on his hind-legs.)

In the Siamese teak forests baby elephants are allowed to run free beside their mothers till they reach the age of five. As soon as one is born—and it must be remembered that teak forest elephants live almost completely natural lives in their natural surroundings, working for only a few hours a day and then grazing in the jungle—a cow elephant from one of the near-by workers attaches itself of its own accord to the mother and becomes the baby's aunt. Thereafter nothing short of force will separate the two cows until the little one is at least three years old. The idea is, I suppose, that, with two

great forms to guard it on either side, the babe
will be well protected from the attacks of tigers, and
the custom, which is presumably the result of instinct,
is a remarkable one known only, as far as I am aware,
to teak-wallahs. A baby elephant, incidentally,
sucks the milk of its mother with mouth, not trunk.

When the youngster is five it is separated by force
from its mother (and " aunt " if still there), and tied
to four stakes in the ground. Against these it strives
uselessly till its spirit is more or less broken and it
learns that man is its master. Every attention and
kindness is then shown it, and a mahout is detailed
off to give it a few simple lessons in being ridden.
To these lessons it usually readily responds.

From the ages of five to fifteen elephants mainly
do baggage work, the howdahs and weights in them
getting bigger along with the growth of the animal.
At fifteen he or she is practically grown-up and can
be put on to timber-work.

The tales that are told of elephants living two or
three hundred years are nonsense. Seventy or eighty
is a good age as with humans, though cases undoubtedly exist of a hundred being reached, while
wild elephants, whose systems have never been
strained dragging heavy logs, probably sometimes
attain a hundred and twenty.

Where do elephants go to when they die? Many
are the stories that have been woven round this
mystery, as mystery to my mind it still is. Wild
elephants are numerous in the north of Siam, yet
never once did I meet a forest hunter or any other
man who had ever come across the remains of one;
which, considering the size of the skeleton, not to

mention the tusks that can never turn to bone dust, is surprising. Personally, I do not believe any burial-ground *does* exist, but further than that I cannot go, preferring to treat the whole question as unanswerable.

Amongst our own force, of course, deaths were fairly frequent, and after cutting out the tusks we made a practice of burning the bodies with kerosene. Diseases in the shape of anthrax and surra accounted for a good many, and occasionally we lost an animal through the bulls fighting one another. As the supply of calves was not sufficient to replace this constant drainage, we bought as and when required from Burmese and Shan elephant traders. These in turn obtained their supply under Government licence by capturing wild elephants and breaking them in. The method of capture has been too often described by other writers for me to go into here, but briefly it is done by rounding up a herd and driving it into a stockade, after which the chosen animals are noosed by tame ones and tied to trees outside the enclosure. They are then put through the ordeal of the posts, which ordeal, remarkably enough, they often take better when fully grown than when they are youngsters. After that it is a matter of training them at baggage and timber-work until they are proficient enough to offer for sale. While I was in Siam a good tusker fetched about six thousand *ticals*, or £600, and a good cow three thousand five hundred.

Cows do not have tusks, but tushes, which are about the size of a boar's tusks. A male elephant generally has two tusks, sometimes only one, and occasionally none (Ceylon provides the exception, for there male elephants for some reason rarely have tusks at all). Males are more valuable for timber-work than females, partly because of their strength, partly because they are not so timid, and partly because their tusks are useful for levering and pushing the logs.

The male has periods of disturbance known as " musth," during which he is highly dangerous and has to remain securely shackled to a tree. One can tell when an attack is coming on by an oily discharge that starts exuding from a hole in the temple; when the oil, which comes out very gradually, has trickled down to a level with the eye—then look out! If he's not properly secured the chances are he'll try to kill anyone in sight.

An elephant cannot take all four feet off the ground at once. In other words, it cannot jump, and a ditch which a horse or even a big dog could cross will therefore stop it completely.

It cannot turn its head round like the average animal because its neck is too short, so if it wants to see what is going on behind, it has to turn its whole body round. This makes it very nervous of being suddenly approached from the rear.

It has an instinctive distrust of dogs and horses, though buffaloes and bullocks it doesn't mind in the least.

With the exception of the whale, it is probably the finest swimmer of all the mammalia.

It is a shade-loving creature, and cannot stand being exposed to hot sun.

It loves getting frightened and starting " panics," especially if a female.

It has such a *thin* skin that it suffers torments from

the bites of insects. For this reason it flings, by the aid of its trunk, dust and mud over itself whenever possible.

If overheated on the march, and there is no water available, it puts its trunk in its mouth, sucks up some spittle, then blows the moisture down the sides of its body. Anyone who has had to walk immediately behind an elephant for any distance in the hot weather quickly discovers this queer habit to his misfortune.

Its sight is not very good, but its powers of scent are enormous. It can wind a man or a tiger up to a distance of over two miles.

It sleeps only for about three hours out of the twenty-four.

So much for generalities. Now for individual characteristics, which vary in elephants just as much as they do in dogs, or in human beings, for that matter. When eventually I was put in charge of our Muang Ngow forest while Orwell went on leave, I found that this was very much the case.

The first elephant to come to my mind is Poo Noi Pee Bah, literally the Small Mad One. Why he was called small I could never understand, for he was a fine, big tusker. For weeks on end he would be a model, working well and behaving well, and then, for no reason connected with " musth " or anything else, he would suddenly become a fierce, morose brute who was liable to get up to any sort of mischief. He would attack other elephants, chase coolies, and one night he attacked the F.M. in his tent, the F.M. being lucky to escape alive. The photograph facing p. 144 is of particular interest, as it was taken only a few hours before this incident occurred; it shows Poo Noi Pee Bah (the elephant in the centre) with the tent behind him.

"I was just falling off to sleep when I heard the chink of hobbles," the F.M. told me one day when showing me the photo, "and remembering Poo Noi Pee Bah's little tricks, I guessed it might be him come to have a go at my tent. I nipped out of bed, seized my electric torch, and went to the entrance. It was dark, but not so dark that you couldn't make out something, and there he was, a great dark shadow coming over the clearing towards the tent. Though it looks all right in the photo, it was beastly slushy and muddy where I was standing, and altogether it wasn't the sort of position I'd care to be in again." Here the F.M. paused reflectively, while I made an unspoken resolve to see that Poo Noi Pee Bah was securely shackled to a tree whenever I had occasion to camp near him.

"He was coming along fast in spite of his hobbles," the F.M. went on, "and I could hear him rumbling, which showed he was in a rage. Didn't like the look of the tent, I suppose. I wanted to switch on my torch, but was afraid if I did, he'd charge me like a shot and give me no chance of reaching the other side of the clearing. So, in spite of mud and snags and goodness knows what, I sprinted over in the dark and reached the coolie lines without falling and without him following me. Minute or two later we'd got hold of the mahout, and Poo Noi Pee Bah was led away just as he was settling down comfortably to smashing up everything I had. . . . Yes, a dangerous brute."

KAMOO COOLIES GIRDLING A TEAK TREE.

Then there was Mae Toom, who always looked in the pink of condition yet who was constantly developing some irritating little minor ailment: a boil, a chain-gall, a sore foot, a chafed trunk, something wrong with one eye. It was as though she did this on purpose to avoid work. Then there were the elephants who loved breaking into villagers' *hais* and devouring their crops, thereby rendering the company liable for many hundreds of *ticals*' worth of damage, and there were those who tried to get free from their hobbles in order to travel afar and join up with wild herds, and there were those who paired into chums.

These " chums " were particularly exasperating. Two, they might be tuskers or they might be cows, would suddenly decide that in the other they had met their soul-mate, and thereafter, as in the " aunt " racket, nothing short of force would separate them. Perhaps one would be a skilled river-worker and the other a hill-worker, necessitating completely different camps being chosen for them, and then the trumpetings, the bellowings, the general rumpus when the separation came! The midnight journeys, too, as they strove to meet again, and the oaths of the mahouts who had to follow them up next day! Still, one couldn't help sympathising with them.

Then there were the killers that were always killers, generally huge, sullen tuskers which, though they had been broken in at the posts, had never really been tamed and still retained the souls of tigers. These had to be employed dragging teak growing far up in the sources of the loneliest creeks, far removed from human habitation and even from

I

other elephants. A rotten job their mahouts had, being buried with them for months on end in God-forsaken surroundings, and one that even if I'd been a Lao I wouldn't have taken on for any money.

The " swaiers " were about the worst type to handle. These refused to have riders on their necks, getting rid of them by sudden, rippling shakes of the neck muscles. The result was that they couldn't do river-work, and when dragging they had to be led by the mahout on foot by means of a piece of rope round the ear—an undignified method of progression.

Then there was the female who would only have the hobbles placed on her hind-legs instead of on the fore, and the " traveller " who insisted on being put in the rear while on the march, and the tusker who loved digging up human corpses and eating them—a disgusting habit but only too painfully true. Obviously, therefore, if a forest was to be run efficiently, one had to get the best out of one's elephants; and to do this the peculiarities of each animal had to be studied so that they could be put on to the work most suited for them. It was as if they said:

" You have conquered me, and I will serve you long and faithfully. But I insist, nevertheless, on retaining one small part of the original me; *this* you will never conquer."

To return to Orwell and Poo Kam Sen, the duel between whom took place whilst I was down south neaping. There was no more modest man than Orwell, consequently the story as he told it me did not do justice to the matchless courage he must have displayed; but I had seen Poo Kam Sen, and I knew every inch of the locality where the scenes were enacted, and was therefore able to read between the lines. The Laos, too, who had been with Orwell at the time, gave me a good many particulars.

Poo Kam Sen went on " musth," and unfortunately broke the chain by which he had been secured to a tree, and got free. Thus it happened that one morning, while travelling on their lawful occasions along a strip of the Nakon–Muang Ngow road, two of our elephants, together with their mahouts, beheld the mightiest tusker in the land advancing upon them, hell in his mien and eye. Even they, the elephants, feared him, and, turning, they fled sideways into the jungle, shedding howdahs and mahouts in the process. Luckily for them, not to speak of the unfortunate men, Poo Kam Sen continued up the road instead of branching aside.

A Lao husbandman, walking alone on the road. He hears a faint sound, the slur of the broken chain, behind him, and casually looks round. A scream of horror rises to his throat, strangles as a mountain surges upon him. He is knocked down, crushed, and left a shapeless mass of flesh and blood on the road.

On then now, mad with " musth " and blood, goes Poo Kam Sen. Except for the very slight chink and slur of the chain, he makes not a sound; that is the terrible thing about him and his kind: he may be a foot or two behind you, and you won't know he's there, so noiselessly does he move.

Nearer and nearer he draws to the village of Muang Ngow. Two bullock-carts appear ahead. The drivers just have time to flee, and he is on them, smashing the carts to matchwood and killing the patient bullocks.

The news flashes around. Poo Kam Sen is loose and has turned killer. Amok, *amok*, AMOK. Orwell, out on a round trip of inspection, hears, foams in to the compound on his grey mare. The scared brown faces, both of his own men and those of the villagers, meet him at the gates. Poo Kam Sen is not Orwell's elephant, but the chief who owns the animal is probably ten days' journey away, and he, Orwell, must be responsible for the safety of the village and its inhabitants.

"Tell everyone to keep to their houses," he snaps to the headman. He next beckons to his own elephant headman; the tuskers of the company are also in danger, for should any of them be seen by Poo Kam Sen the chances are they will be attacked outright.

"Have every *Poo* that is near the village sent a good ten miles away."

The headman salaams, flees to see the orders carried out.

Orwell strides out of the compound, remounts the grey mare, gallops through the village, watched anxiously by the people in their flimsy shanties, and, reaching the ford, goes gingerly along the Mae Ngow bank. The dry weather has started, so the river is at low level.

Suddenly a bomb seems to burst on his left. Poo Kam Sen, hiding unseen in the fringing jungle, must be charging him. Orwell wheels the grey mare in a quicker turn than ever she did at polo, and gallops furiously back up the bank. At the ford he swings round in the saddle, but no menacing, balloon-like shape is following him. Going back cautiously—

and this is no easy task, for the mare is dancing with fear—he eventually discovers that Poo Kam Sen has also flown in terror from *them*, for he is in full retreat down the almost dry river-bed.

Poo Kam Sen stops his flight, turns, glares balefully at Orwell on the prancing mare. Already he is recovering from the scare given him by the sudden sight and smell of horse, and it is only a matter of seconds before he will charge again. But Orwell does not wait; he has seen what he wanted to: the flow of oil down the temple, and, knowing Poo Kam Sen really is on " musth," he swings the mare round yet again and gallops hell-for-leather for the compound.

Back there, he flings himself into a long cane chair in his bungalow, and thinks furiously. Poo Kam Sen has become a rogue, and, the law of Siam being that rogues can and should be shot at sight, he should suffer that fate before any more men are killed or property is damaged. *But*—— Orwell is a man who loves elephants and would not willingly take the life of one. He dwells on Poo Kam Sen's matchless strength and mighty grandeur. Shall *he* be the man to lay low such magnificence, when in the course of two or three weeks' time the " musth " will in all probability have passed, leaving Poo Kam Sen as harmless as the very bullocks he has slain?

Somehow he must trap Poo Kam Sen, then noose him and have him dragged to where he can be secured to a tree. But how to trap the Colossus in the first place? At last, when the light is failing, Orwell gets an idea.

Night falls, an uneasy night for the whole village, with that great death lurking on the outskirts.

Dawn. Orwell goes to the office, summons the village headman, his own chief headman, and some of his coolies and mahouts. He points to a strip of harvested paddyland opposite the company compound on the other side of the river.

"Dig a pit," he tells them, "there, in the centre of that field. Let it be nine feet deep and six feet wide, and let every man available get on with the work. When the pit is finished, conceal it with a covering of leaves and bamboo, then place a plank across the middle so that a man may get over in safety and an elephant may not."

"So," murmurs the brown audience, puzzled but vastly interested.

"When everything is ready," Orwell continues, "the mahouts shall drive two cow elephants into the field in the hopes of luring Poo Kam Sen after them."

"But the pit," objects the village headman. "Of what use is it, master? For it will only be by the merest chance that Poo Kam Sen will go near enough to fall into it."

"It will not be by the merest chance," returns Orwell, "because a man will go into the middle of the field, and the elephant, seeing him, will charge. The man will then make for the pit and run across the plank, leaving Poo Kam Sen to . . . surely it is clear?"

"Meh," exclamations of awe rise from a dozen dusky throats. "And who . . . who will be the man, master?"

"I will be," says Orwell, and grins.

.　　　.　　　.　　　.　　　　　.

Thus it came about that the pit was dug, the females driven into position, and Poo Kam Sen lured out after them into the middle of the field. Behind the pit, armed with bamboo spears and ropes, stood numerous mahouts and coolies. And with them was Orwell.

" I'm going," said he, after a final glance round at the preparations. Then, perhaps a little white of face, he walked half-way down one side of the field, after which he swung boldly out into the open.

Poo Kam Sen, dallying with his cows, saw him, let out one great bellow of wrath, surged his whole colossal bulk forward to blot out this impudent pigmy. Orwell, turning, fled for his life towards the pit.

He had worked it all out beforehand; he was a good sprinter, and knew that in *open* ground a man, provided he has a reasonable start, can keep ahead of a charging elephant for, at any rate, a short distance; and he had, he thought, judged time and distance to a nicety.

But had he? Would the pit *never* be reached? On and on he ran, with the great death swinging along behind him. He made to turn his head, but in so doing tripped over a tuft of stubble and nearly fell, at which his heart started hammering perilously. One fall—and all would be over for him.

Poo Kam Sen was gaining on him, gaining, gaining; though he dared not turn round, he was *sure* of it. Ah, there was the concealed pit—at last, and there the plank leading to safety. One, two, three, four—and he was over.

Crash! With a thud that literally shook the earth the vast body smashed down into the pit.

"Quick! The ropes!" pants Orwell.

The coolies and mahouts leap forward, their object being to secure Poo Kam Sen's legs and thus render him helpless against the company elephants that will shortly arrive to drag him to a tree; but the awesome spectacle of the huge leviathan, bellowing and trumpeting and rumbling and bubbling, smashing and heaving and goring at the sides of his prison, causes their hands to tremble and the ropes to get confused.

"Out. He's getting out!" suddenly shrieks one of the men.

A pause, in which, to their horror, they see that Poo Kam Sen, thanks to his stupendous might, has actually managed to tear down part of one side of the pit and is beginning to heave himself up over the falling earth. Up he comes, up, up . . . then the coolies and mahouts wait for no more. Dropping their ropes, they flee in terror across the Mae Ngow river. Orwell, finding himself alone and helpless, has no course left him but to follow them.

The party gain the further bank of the river and run up into the company compound. There they see Poo Kam Sen sullenly rolling off into the jungle beyond the paddy-fields. But the fall has evidently shaken him, for he walks with a limp.

That evening news comes that he has killed another man.

There followed for the village, indeed for the whole district, nights and days of fear, a fear augmented one particular night by thieves dragging a chain through a darkened alley-way, thereby inducing the populace of Muang Ngow to believe that the killer was in their midst, and causing them to make a mad dash from the market-place. Once the stalls were clear of occupants, the thieves, with smiles upon their faces, emerged from the alley-way and helped themselves to whatever they wanted. Poetic justice should have decreed that as they were doing this Poo Kam Sen actually *did* turn up and killed them, but unfortunately these gentlemen lived on to enjoy their ill-gotten gains.

Owing to the menace of the killer the work of the whole Muang Ngow teak forest came to a standstill; those of the Laos who were employed in distant, safe corners of the forest came in to the village to see the fun, while those who were employed near the village rushed off to the forest to get away from it; as for Orwell himself, he was far too busy trying to trap the cause of the trouble to be able to straighten things out.

At last there came to Orwell the company's elephant-medicine-maker, bearing a bundle of arrows, the tips of which were stained with a greenish fluid, and a buffalo horn filled with powder.

" Lord," said he, " I have an idea. These are poisoned arrows, and if they are put in guns and fired at Poo Kam Sen's legs, then will he become so lame that he will scarcely be able to move at all; at which your servants the coolies and mahouts will surely have the chance to rope him."

Orwell jumped at the suggestion. He had his own gun, and the somewhat primitive fire-arms belonging to the village headman and one or two others, loaded

with the arrows, then the party went off stalking Poo
Kam Sen. They came across him, half in and half
out of the jungle on the river-bank below the ford,
and though Orwell tried to restrain his followers till
they were at closer quarters, the sight of the great
beast was too much for them; off went the guns,
nearly killing Orwell in the process and causing Poo
Kam Sen to bolt without a scratch.

After that Orwell decided to hunt alone. What
happened during the next few days only he knows,
but he was successful in getting several arrows home,
and it wasn't long before Poo Kam Sen was reduced
to impotency.

" It was a ghastly sight, though, in the end," concluded Orwell. " The great brute was rolling and
staggering like a drunken man, what with the pain
of the poison and the ' musth ' going out of him.
Wasn't even necessary to get elephants to drag him
to a tree; his mahout eventually came along and he
obeyed him like a lamb. Will he get over it, did
you say? He was almost himself again by the time
I left to come in here."

Thus ended the running amok of Poo Kam Sen.
And if ever a man showed courage and resource in
a trying time, with no one to help him and a great
responsibility upon his shoulders, it was Orwell.

It is with the deepest regret that I have just heard,
while writing this book, of his death in his native
Gloucestershire. There was valour and no meanness
in him.

## CHAPTER TEN

# THUNDERSTORM

WHILE in Nakon I sold my black pony, which had turned out rather a useless animal, and in its place what did I buy? I rebought Sunstar from the missionary! The missionary seemed pleased to be rid of him, and for some extraordinary reason I felt every bit as pleased to have him back. He was quieter than he had been before, and when I came to ride the odd fifty miles out to Muang Ngow, whither the F.M. was sending me to do a few odd jobs, we got along famously. Even the sight of another pony, though setting him dancing a bit, did not have quite the disastrous results of yore.

After a short stay in the Muang Ngow forest, during which I inspected exhausted areas—an awful job, consisting of beating through mile upon mile of worked-out jungle to see if the felling headman had left any logs behind—I was summoned back to Nakon in order to go on down to another forest of ours a little to the south of Nakon called the Mae Tah.

On the evening of the third day of the journey back from Muang Ngow, the day on which I was due to camp in the temple referred to in Chapter II, I noticed a dense black cloud piling up in the southwest. The day had been one of terrific heat, and, seeing that a first-class thunderstorm seemed likely to be terminating it, I felt thankful that we were going to camp in the temple instead of in the ordinary jungle clearing. To get in before the storm broke, I pushed Sunstar on ahead of my transport, little Sclave following gamely at his heels.

I arrived at Sadet, the village close by the temple, when the storm appeared to be poised right over us. The Mae Wang river, no longer in flood as it had been on that first journey of mine out from Nakon to Muang Ngow, looked a bilious yellow under the livid clouds, while the jungle that hemmed in the village and fringed the further bank was extraordinarily quiet; not a bird called, not a beast rustled through the undergrowth; Nature seemed holding her breath.

At the entrance guarded by the red-mouthed dragons I dismounted and, flinging Sunstar's reins to my pony-boy, who had been following me on the red, told him to find quick shelter for himself and the ponies. I then, followed by Sclave, passed through the gates and entered the temple compound. Not a whisper of wind stirred, and my lungs were gasping for lack of air. From head to foot I was soaked in sweat; I had sweated whilst riding Sunstar along the heat-shimmering road; I sweated now that I was walking. Simply to raise a hand was sufficient to make one sweat.

I entered the temple, to encounter slightly cooler air. The bronze Buddha still stared grimly ahead of it with unwinking eyes, but the tinsel ornaments in the roof were for once silent for lack of a draught. Bathed in my oily sweat I sat down on the flagged floor to wait for the rain to begin, and hoped that my kit, which was following up on two slow bullock-carts (we never employed baggage elephants in the hot weather), wouldn't get too wet.

Half an hour passed without incident. I rose, leaving a damp patch on the flags where I had been sitting, and went outside. Still the storm hovered right overhead, covering the whole of the western half of the sky. Though a full hour had to elapse before the setting of the sun, it had grown very dark; the storm centre was a dull, dead black, while to the east the sky was palish blue, cloud-free yet subdued in tone as though aware of coming catastrophe. A flock of parrakeets, followed by a flock of minas, flew by, seeking their nests and crying as if in alarm. No villagers were about, and when the birds disappeared the silence was so intense that it seemed to buzz.

Suddenly there came fluffs of hot wind, then fluffs of slightly cooler wind which beat welcomingly about my cheeks. At the same time I heard groans and squeaks, and my bullocks lurched into the clearing by the temple compound. The carts had travelled (for them) at an amazingly fast pace, but the drivers, with their eyes on the storm, had evidently lashed the patient bullocks out of their usual slow walk. Behind the carts came my carrier coolies and servants.

The fluffs of wind increased in strength, and very soon I heard a sullen roar, like the roaring of many distant waterfalls, approaching from the south-west; it was the roar of the wind and rain coming up over the trees. I yelled to the men to get a move on unloading the carts, then bolted for the shelter of the temple.

Before I reached it the storm was upon us. I saw a tall coconut tree spring up and down as though pulled by the fingers of some gigantic passing hand, and simultaneously a flood of ice enveloped me, causing me to gasp; doubtless both rain and wind were warm enough in reality, but after the sweltering heat of the last few hours they felt as cold as death.

When I reached the temple the tinkling ornaments were dancing like mad, for the temple had no door and the wind was surging up and down between the walls. As I stood there, my hair lifting, my boy staggered through the murk with a bundle of my kit.

"The blankets," I shouted to him above the crashing of the rain, my one thought being to guard against an attack of malaria by getting off my sweat-sodden clothes. "Never mind about anything else. Get the blankets, then run for the shelter of the *sala*, and stay there."

"The blankets, they here, master," yelled my boy, who was a good lad. "They here in this bundle."

"Right," I told him. "Now get back to shelter where the others are."

He vanished into the gloom. It turned completely dark. Fumbling and cursing, my teeth chattering with that cold wind penetrating my wet clothing, I opened the bundle and pulled out the soft, welcome warmth of my camp-bed blankets. These I wrapped round me after tearing off my other garments, and then, with shoulders hunched like any native mendicant, I squatted down on the remains of the bundle.

I hadn't been sitting thus for more than five minutes when the wind dropped as suddenly as it had started. The rain, however, continued heavier than ever, and since it was now descending vertically it fairly crashed on to the temple roof.

It was while I was listening to it that the flash came, such a flash as is inconceivable. It seemed to sear my eyeballs, to *hurt* me so that my whole body quivered. I could smell it, too, for it brought with it the sort of whiff you get when passing an underground station in London, and I could hear it, for it sizzled. A split second later the whole sky was splintered with such a crash of thunder that I rocked on the bundle and felt as though my skull had been pole-axed.

I think for several moments I must have sat there half-dazed (I heard later from my servants that the lightning seemed to strike the earth immediately in front of the temple), and the first things I remember clearly afterwards are feeling the cold thrust of Sclave's nose and hearing his whimper above the thrumming of the rain. The poor little chap was trembling all over, as well he might have been, and I drew him into my blankets.

The thunderstorm proper began. There were no more flashes of the severity of the first, but they were quite bad enough, and the thunder was absolutely continuous; first there came the crash, then the echoes of it went rolling round the sky in gigantic reverberations which had not ceased before the next crash arrived and set them rolling afresh. The lightning was ridiculously like that in a stage storm: flicker, flicker, flicker—pause—flicker, flicker, flicker—pause; and with the grim figure of Buddha on his pedestal appearing and reappearing in time with the lightning, the scene was most eerie.

I suppose I ought to have felt frightened, but instead a tremendous exhilaration was mine. I felt fey, mad with the splendour of it all, so much so that every now and then I raised my puny voice and shouted back at the thunder. A man had once told me that while taking part in a big attack on the Western Front his main sensation was being drunk—drunk with excitement, and now I could well believe him. Here too was drum-fire, heaven's drum-fire.

Gradually the storm weakened as it passed over to the east, and at last the thunderous blare of noise died away, leaving only a thin rain in its wake and the mournful drip, drip, drip of countless trees. A wan light, the last faint gleam of real light before the real dark, relieved the utter blackness, and my boy appeared, carrying a lamp and followed by a coolie with my table.

The pair sploshed through the flooded compound, entered the temple, set up the table and lit the lamp.

" The master will take his wisaky now? " the boy demanded, without the ghost of an expression on his face.

Of a truth he was the perfect butler!

It seems strange now as I write these words, with the hum of my next-door neighbour's lawn-mower in my ears and all the comforts of civilisation within my reach (I do not say pocket), that once I crouched, clad only in blankets and with only a dog for company, beneath an Eastern image in an Eastern temple fringed by jungle and mantled in the flare and blare of an Eastern thunderstorm. But that is the joy of such contrasts, which go far to adding zest to life.

.        .        .        .        .        .

POO NOI PEE BAH, THE KILLER (CENTRE), TAKEN SHORTLY BEFORE HE ATTACKED THE TENT IN THE PICTURE, NEARLY KILLING THE TEAK-WALLAH IN IT.

I arrived safely in Nakon the next day, then continued on south, part of the way by train, till I came to the forest of the Mae Tah.

Here I stayed two months, and dull I found them, because the forest was dull. Why is one street boring to one man and interesting to another? One cannot explain. But to me the Muang Ngow forest was always full of interest, while the very reverse applied to the Mae Tah, partly I suppose because the latter was the smaller of the two. The chief reason though, I think, was that the Mae Tah had no *character* about it; it just left one cold.

The only exciting incident I remember there was seeing a wild dog attack a sambhur. I was tramping along the bank of the Mae Tah river at a point where its right bank was very low and its left, the one on which I was, very high—a good twenty feet above the level of the bed. The hot weather was at its peak, consequently the bed consisted of nothing but sandbanks in between which there meandered a dry watercourse of shining stones and patches of sand and gravel. The only water anywhere was an occasional pool, and it was in one of these pools, close up under the high bank on which I was walking, that I beheld a sambhur, drinking.

To see any wild creature in its natural environment, completely oblivious of man and of the fact that it is being watched, possesses extraordinary fascination, and in order to make myself as inconspicuous as possible, I lay flat down on the bank and peered cautiously over the rim. Sclave, who was with me, I held by the collar, and though he knew something was " up " by my behaviour, he hadn't winded the

K

deer and was luckily keeping quiet. Except for Sclave, I was completely alone, for my transport was well behind me.

The sambhur, a beautiful stag, well-pointed, stood knee-deep in the pool with his muzzle down to the water. As I watched him placidly drinking—he was evidently in no hurry and enjoying the coolness—a sudden flash of colour and movement at the rim of the yellow, burnt-out jungle on the flat bank opposite caught my attention, and, taking my eyes off the deer, I saw a wild dog emerge from the jungle and make straight over the sand-banks for the pool. It was of the ordinary type that looks rather like a cross between· a pariah dog and an English fox, being red-brown in colour and having a thick, bushy tail.

Arrived within a few yards of the pool it stopped its forward course and, obviously in a state of great excitement, started pacing to and fro in front of the pool in exactly the same way as one sees the carnivora in the Zoo pacing behind their bars just before feeding time. And though the dog was almost within striking distance of him, that sambhur never noticed its arrival, but went on calmly drinking. In view of the fact that the two are natural enemies, this sounds almost incredible, but I saw it with my own eyes, and I heard later that another teak-wallah had seen the same sort of thing.

Normally wild dogs hunt in packs; indeed, it is obvious from their size that they must do so if they want to pull down anything, and I glanced along the flat bank opposite for signs of the new arrival's pals. But the jungle slept on in the brilliant sunshine, and it was apparent that our friend was a lone specimen that was daring enough to seek out and beard even a mighty stag.

At last the sambhur ceased drinking, lifted his head —and saw the dog. Thereafter things happened with celerity. I heard a coughing grunt, the water of the pool frothed as the stag leapt out of it, then with lowered head he was charging over the tiny space of intervening sand.

I expected the dog to turn and flee, but instead it slithered sideways from the rush, then stood its ground and faced its aggressor.

The fight was on. Again and again the stag charged, only to be eluded with ease. Never once did the dog try to attack, but if it were hoping to wear out the other, it struck me that it would tire just as quickly, for the heat on the sand was tremendous and the dog, being shorter of leg, would feel it most.

After a little while the pair worked round so that they disappeared from my view behind a solitary, hardy, evergreen bush that grew out of the sand. I was still bound to see how the combat ended, for before reaching the jungle they still had to cross the large stretch of sand-bank that lay between the jungle and the bush; nevertheless, that bush came in for a good deal of cursing on my part; for tantalising grunts and little fluffs of sand kicked up by the sambhur's hooves kept coming out from behind it, letting me know that the duel was still on but not telling me how it was going.

At last I could stand the suspense no longer. Even though it would end the fight, I decided to slither down the bank and rush round behind the bush.  But I couldn't let Sclave come with me in case he chose to join in the scrap and got injured or killed, and I was looking to see whether I could tie his collar to anything, when I *felt* rather than heard a rush of movement across the sand in the direction of the jungle opposite.  Casting aside all concealment now, and with Sclave following me, I scrambled down the steep bank, nearly breaking my neck in the process, and on reaching the bottom raced across to the bush. Save for hoof-marks in the sand, marks that were rapidly filling in, not a sign of the recent duel existed, either behind the bush itself or over the sand-bank leading to the jungle.  Were it not for my own eyes and those rapidly disappearing hoof-marks, the whole affair might have been part of a dream.

I often wonder how the fight ended; probably, I should imagine, by the dog breaking it off and running. But perhaps they're still at it, a ghostly dog and a ghostly sambhur, chasing each other for ever and ever through a silent and ghostly jungle.

Based on the various scraps I saw between different kinds of animals in Siam, I hold the theory that when animals fight—I say " fight " as opposed to mere killing as a tiger kills a deer—they make a tremendous amount of noise and a great display of ferocity in order to intimidate each other.  Thus a fight that *seems* very bloodthirsty may continue for a considerable time without the least damage being done on either side.  When a fight *does* go on to the death, therefore (I refer, of course, to fairly evenly-matched com-batants), the savagery of the spectacle must be sickeningly revolting.  A teak-wallah in another firm, for instance, told me that a tiger attacked a big, strong water-buffalo near his camp one evening, and that the fight went on *all night* before the buffalo was slain. A buffalo, in spite of its bulk, can only produce, apart from a snort, the faintest of bleats, but the noise the tiger made, he said, was indescribably awful. I myself was later to hear a duel between a tiger and an elephant, and though it took place over a mile away from me the sound was pretty alarming.

I remember nothing more of those two months in the Mae Tah forest save that I was becoming increasingly aware of stomach troubles. Since they had first started in the Mae Lah, to be followed by a severe bout of colic at that pleasant watering-place Sukothai, I had never been really free from them, and now they were growing severe; I could not take a meal without paying for it, and I had lost a good deal of weight. I resolved to see a Bangkok doctor when the opportunity came, and I thought with some trepidation of the numbers of teak-wallahs who had been invalided home in the past.

At the beginning of July, when the rains had been on some weeks, I received orders to go down to Sawankaloke, R.S. No. 1, in order to take over the whole of the company's rafting that year. No big main river rise had occurred as yet, I was informed, but one might happen any week now, and I was to be in Sawankaloke in readiness for it. I thankfully left the monotonous Mae Tah forest, which dripped mournfully under the grey monsoon rain, and, after arranging for my ponies to be sent into Nakon, caught the southbound train for Bangkok, for here was my opportunity to see that doctor.

" Sounds as if you were suffering from the after-effects of dysentery," said he, when he had listened to my story. "Sure you never had dysentery before you came out to Siam?"

"Quite sure," I answered.

"You were through the War, weren't you?"

I nodded.

"Sure you didn't get anything then? Where were you?"

I told him: English Channel, Dardanelles, Salonika, Ægean generally, and lastly, for my sins, an awful place not a hundred miles from the Firth of Forth.

"Humph. Gallipoli," he said doubtfully. "Lot of dysentery there, you know."

"There was," I agreed. "But we in the ships weren't bothered with it much."

"Must be ordinary digestive troubles," he diagnosed after a pause, "brought on by bad food and the climate. Now I want you to cut out tea altogether and to take these . . ." And he handed me a prescription.

So back I went up the line to Wang Mai Korn, bound for Sawankaloke, tea-less and the proud possessor of a bottle of pepsin, bismuth and charcoal tablets, disgusting things that when chewed made one's mouth as black as the inside of any Northumbrian coal-pit. But the treatment had some effect, temporarily at any rate, as for a few weeks I felt much better.

No rise had occurred when I reached Sawankaloke, so there was nothing to do but wait for one. And when I say "nothing" I mean it; there was nothing, nothing, nothing to occupy the attention in Sawan-

kaloke. To begin with, I was the only white man
there, my Danish friends having left for another
locality, and as the country all round consisted of
nothing but flat ground covered with gigantically tall
elephant-grass, one couldn't even go for solitary
walks. As if to make the monotony worse, a thick
drizzle fell continuously which, while quite useless for
flooding the river and causing the logs to come down,
made everything as damp and depressing as could be.

In all I waited four weeks for that rise to happen,
and how I got through them I don't know. I'd get
up as late as was decently possible, linger over breakfast and a post-breakfast cigarette, drift down to the
office, which was directly beneath the bungalow, find
with an effort perhaps half an hour's work by paying
some raftsmen who wanted advances, or by rationing
them out some cane, and then, since walking was out
of the question, up the steps I'd go again to the
bungalow. It probably wanted at least another
two hours before tiffin, and I'd start playing the
gramophone I had and which invariably accompanied me wherever I went. I hadn't too many
records, but these were used over and over again,
particularly one called "The Gipsy Warned Me."
How often Violet Loraine must have sung that song
out over the depressing, drizzle-enshrouded river I
cannot imagine; but her lovely voice brought back
visions of when I had sat, entranced, and listened to
her singing "Some Girl has got to Darn his Socks,"
in "Round the Map." Though she had worn glasses
and was dressed in a black shawl, she had held that
crowded audience of khaki and blue so that one could
have heard the proverbial pin drop, and, sitting in

that bungalow and listening to " The Gipsy Warned Me," I could see and hear her again as plainly as in those hectic War days.

After an hour or two of the gramophone I'd eat a heavy tiffin, then fall into a heavy sleep. Oh, the joy of waking up about four o'clock in the sticky heat of the bedroom, one's skin all oily, one's mouth like a chemical factory, and with the knowledge that one couldn't have a cup of tea! I just longed for tea then, and found coffee a poor, almost nauseating substitute at that time of the day.

In the evening I strolled round the compound if the drizzle wasn't too thick, idly looking at nothing in particular and followed by Sclave, who also seemed bored. Things livened up, however, when on one of these strolls he encountered a " tokay " lizard on the ground, a particularly fat, big specimen a good foot and a half long, resembling a miniature dragon. Every time Sclave made a feint at it, it swung round and presented a formidable array of needle-sharp, snapping teeth at him. But he kept on attacking (*he* was no coward), and at last managed to seize it across the back, whereupon he shook it exactly as a terrier shakes a rat; the force a dog can put into this action is astonishing, and the " tokay " didn't survive the treatment more than half a minute.

After dinner I'd read the advertisements in the last batch of newspapers out from England (the news I had probably read long ago), then after a period of general mooning around, and a last vain glance at the Mae Yome for signs of a rise, I'd turn in. I was so bored I hadn't even the heart to summon my phantom naval friends, for they'd have been bored too. And I was too bored to take to solitary drinking. Hobbies? I tried to think of some, but couldn't.

The only changes from the general monotony were several slight goes of low fever I experienced. Malaria has many ways of coming out in a man; usually it brings a high temperature and ague, and can then be very dangerous. It was the fate of most teak-wallahs to have at least one bad bout which they were lucky to survive, but I myself never went in for anything worse than low fever as opposed to high. I generally felt it coming on in the evening; all day I'd be feeling tired and out of sorts, and about five o'clock the calves of the legs would begin to ache, the eyelids to sting, the head and nose to feel stuffy, and curious little, trickling shivers would come creeping over the skin, like cat's-paws of wind over sea. The skin also would be hot and dry, and I'd know for sure what I was in for.

Here is a typical Low Fever Evening in Sawan-kaloke:

" Boy! " I shout, " *ow heep yah mah.*"

In comes the boy, carrying my medicine-chest, a little tin box partitioned off for the various bottles of Burroughs and Wellcome tabloids. I take out fifteen grains of quinine and ten of aspirin, and swallow them with the aid of some lukewarm, filtered water.

" I'm going to bed," I say to the boy. " Light the lamp in the bedroom and bring blankets."

" Yes, master."

I walk from the living-room to the stuffy bedroom. Those shivers are trickling more and more over my skin, and though my brain is strangely active, I feel very tired physically. " I must bring on a sweat," I say to myself. " Then this confounded fever will go."

I slip off my day kit, which consists of khaki shorts and a white cotton shirt, and then, instead of putting on the usual night rig—black Chinese trousers and singlet—I don the thickest pair of pyjama trousers I can find, a flannel tennis shirt, a pair of thick socks, and a sweater. Clad now like a boxing instructor, but feeling very much unlike one, I get into bed, and on top of this already warm kit heap the blankets the boy brings me. The bed is a big square affair, part of the bungalow furniture, and I lie in the middle of it, with the blankets wrapped round me so that not even an elbow or finger is visible. I now have to await the coming of the sweat.

The two oil-lamps, one set on a table and one hanging from the ceiling, light the dark, wooden-walled room but dimly. Staring straight ahead of me, I see lizards crawling along the walls; most of them are little " chin-chocks," but one is a huge " tokay," and I watch him stalking a moth that has settled near him. Inch by inch he approaches it, first one scaly leg going out in front of him and then the other, and at last, when my nerves are almost at breaking point with suspense, there is a sudden jump, a snapping of teeth, and the moth is no more. Even into this room the law of the jungle has penetrated.

The noises of the night come faintly in through the open window: the hoot of an owl, the squeak of an otter, the faint breathing of the river. Then all minor sounds are drowned by the howling of a dog from the village near by. The howl is taken up by another dog, and another, and another. Soon every pariah in the hamlet is voicing his lament to the weeping skies. Now high, now low, now long-drawn-out and now in sobbing intermissions, goes the weirdly melancholy ululation, and I muse on the Lao saying: " When the dogs howl, a spirit is passing."

It is strange how, in spite of the eerie night, I do not feel lonely. No white man is within fifty miles of me, yet I don't yearn to be back in a town. I wonder why this is.

Curse this sweat. Won't it ever come? I have been lying here for ages, with body simply on fire, yet I am still as dry as a bone all over.

" Boy! " I shout.

" Yes, master." His dusky face emerges from the gloom in the outer passage, his bare, dusky feet making a faint whisper over the hard, teak boards.

" Bring me some hot water," I order, and he vanishes.

That ought to make me sweat, if I can gulp it down quickly enough. Tea would have been nicer, though: lovely, hot tea. I'd give a fortune for a cup of tea, but in view of the doctor's orders I daren't tell the boy to make one. Or dare I? I am still debating the point when the boy reappears with the hot water, and shudderingly I gulp down the nauseating stuff.

More waiting, interminable waiting. Then suddenly I am aware of something running down my chest like a tiny, warm ball. Then another starts, coming from nowhere, going to nowhere. Ha! the sweat has started, and I wriggle in pleasurable anticipation.

Now it fairly bursts out on me, but I make no movement to free myself of the blankets until it is like lying in an oil-bath. Then:

" Boy," I yell.

" Yes, master."

" Bring me a towel, then change the bedding and turn the mattress."

The towel is produced. I get out of bed, retreat to one corner, and, while the boy goes about his task, tear off my sodden things and dry rapidly, for I must take care that I don't get a chill and thus make my last estate worse than the first.

Back in bed again, a bed now cool and dry and wholesome, and with a good deal of the fever wrung out of me, I feel a whole heap better.

Thus a Low Fever Evening in Sawankaloke. And it might have been worse; it might have been a Low Fever Evening in Sukothai.

·     ·     ·     ·     ·

Eventually, after a day and night of terrific rain, the Mae Yome had a thundering rise. Teak logs rode down by the thousand, and never was work more welcome than that into which I plunged. When the rise was at its height I walked up to the big waterfall four miles above Sawankaloke, and fine it was to see the logs spinning over it and toppling down into the boiling water beneath. The journey back I did in a dug-out paddled by skilled boatmen—an exhilarating experience. Borne on the breast of the mighty flood, we made terrific going, and I was wondering where all the big islands in the centre of the river-bed had gone to, when swirling eddies and snags of all kinds racing past our bows made me realise that we were going right *over* them. Such a rise—over twenty feet in a few hours—is almost inconceivable to those accustomed only to our patient English rivers.

In due course the rafts were made up and I went down to R.S. No. 2 at Sukothai. Here again, thanks be, I was obliged to work morning, noon and hot and sticky night, and then, shaking the mud of the dismal place thankfully off my feet, I continued on down to R.S. No. 3 at Paknampoh.

I had only been a fortnight there when I heard that a teak-wallah who was more or less permanently based on Sukothai had been attacked by dacoits only a few days after I had left. He was in camp in some flat jungle behind the town—his firm, unlike mine, had some teak growing in the locality—and on hearing a rumpus going on in his cook's tent had marched out of his in order to ascertain the trouble. To his horror he found that a party of dacoits was raiding the camp and intimidating his servants. On seeing him one of the dacoits dropped on one knee and, aiming a somewhat primitive gun at him, pulled the trigger before he had time to move. The weapon, however, by the sheerest piece of luck, missfired, and the teak-wallah was able to rush back to his tent and seize his revolver. With this he drove the cravens off, but it must have been a nerve-shattering experience for him, and what with that and the tragedy already related in this book, I felt gladder than ever to be out of the Sukothai district.

Soon after I arrived at Paknampoh my digestive troubles recommenced in a more violent form. I went through agonies with them for the whole of the two months it took me to get the rafts through the Royalty Stations, then about Christmas time I went on down to Bangkok to see the doctor again. This time he put me in a nursing home " for observation."

Directly I got in the home my troubles completely vanished, and I felt better than I had done for a very long time. This is the sort of thing that *will* happen; when at last you *do* get a chance of attention, the symptoms seem to know and hide themselves so as not to give the doctor a clue. With a different kind of dope, therefore, and with the doctor still mystified, off I returned to the north.

As on the previous year, I did first the neap of the Mae Yome above Sawankaloke, after which I was detailed off for the two-hundred-and-twenty-mile neap from Nakon to Paknampoh. As I have already mentioned, this was a very lonely journey, far removed from the railway line and other marks of civilisation, and my stomach demon was fully aware of the fact. He waited till I was well down the Mae Wang river and nearing its mouth, that is, until I was almost half-way to Paknampoh, then struck in an effort, not merely to hurt me, but to finish me off altogether.

## CHAPTER ELEVEN

# HOME ON SICK LEAVE

Two days and nights of the stomach demon's offensive effectively stopped me from neaping, and there was nothing to do but pitch camp in the shade on the river bank. This I did about a day's journey north of where the Mae Wang ran into the Mae Ping, in an extra lonely stretch of country, with only one small jungle village about five miles from my camp. I then put myself to bed.

The attacks increased in severity, and soon I could take no solids at all, while even liquids like Bovril or watered condensed milk doubled me up. In spite of this, I did not feel in the least bit terrified, I suppose because I was far too busy being ill to bother about anything else. I had also no hope of any help coming, and it's hope that distracts a man and sets his brain peering this way and that with worry. The quickest way of getting into communication with the outside world would be to send coolies on down to Raheng, the one and only native town in the district a day's journey down the Mae Ping below the mouth of the Mae Wang; there, at Raheng, a telegram could be despatched either to Nakon or to Bangkok, but it would take a good ten days for aid to arrive from either of the latter two places (a fortnight from the date of the coolies actually leaving me), and in my condition I could not visualise such a length of time. So I just stayed put in the tent.

On the fourth or fifth morning in camp the spasms suddenly left me, and in their place a most perfect sensation stole over me. I seemed to be floating in a lovely purple sea, which soothed the nerves and gave one a feeling of exquisite languor. Time and space vanished. There was just me and that purple sea.

Idly, as in some opium dream, I saw little Sclave on the ground-sheet beside my bed. At the moment he didn't seem to be actually *on* the sheet; he just seemed suspended over the purple sea, and as my drugged eyes rested on him, his tail wagged and he smiled. What would happen to him, I idly wondered, when I . . . when I . . .

I emerged from the sea in a flash. The realities of my tent encircled me. I raised myself up on one elbow on the bed. When I . . . when I *what*? How had that question come to me, and what was the missing word?

I *knew* the missing word.

There had I been, calmly lying down—a-dying. To hell with dying!

" Boy! " I yelled.

" Yes, master."

" Bring me eggs and Bovril and milk," I told him when he arrived from the cook's tent.

I had eaten absolutely nothing for the last two days; the resultant spasms hadn't been worth it. But now I would, I must. I swung my feet to the ground and stood up. Considering everything, it was surprising that I didn't feel a good deal more

ELEPHANT KEEPING LOGS ON THE MOVE IN A RISE.

shaky. But thin? I had been thin for months, and now I was positively a skeleton. Well, the skeleton must travel.

I forced down what the boy brought me, to pay for it in the usual manner. But at least I was retaining a little nourishment to help me along, and I then set about working out a programme.

Two days' journey would bring me to Raheng, and there I would send telegrams both to the F.M. in Nakon and to the G.M. in Bangkok, stating that my health had broken down and that on arrival in Paknampoh I was continuing on down to Bangkok instead of doubling back to Nakon. I would stay, I decided, a day or two in Raheng to rest my men and to give myself the comfort of a bungalow. One of the British teak firms had a station there, and though I knew that the European in charge would be absent at this time of the year, it was an understood thing among us teak-wallahs that we could always use each other's premises. On leaving Raheng there would still be, of course, roughly a ten-day journey down the Mae Ping before I reached Paknampoh and the railway, and I would have to trust to luck that my strength kept up sufficiently to complete it, otherwise . . .

I quickly switched my brain off the " otherwise " to consider how the logs had better be counted, for I would be too weak to walk over the gruelling sand-banks. It seemed a pity, now that half the neap was done, that another teak-wallah should have to make a special journey to complete it, and I decided to let my servants help me along the short stretch of the Mae Wang neap still remaining should any walking be found necessary, while as for the Mae Ping, my clerks ought to be awaiting me, reliable men who should be quite capable of doing the count on their own provided I kept an eye on them.

I called to my boy, gave him the necessary directions, the tents were taken down and put in the big boat, I placed myself in the dug-out, and we shoved off. Luckily there was very little timber on the final stretches of the Mae Wang, and at the mouth sure enough there were my Siamese clerks.

The following day, in the evening of which we were due at Raheng, I very soon tired of being stewed alive in the dug-out. If one has got to be fully exposed to the sun, I've always found it preferable to take exercise so that one may sweat freely in it (how people grill themselves for hour after hour on the English beaches nowadays beats me, though it's good for the doctors owing to the number of nerve complaints it brings for them to cure), so out of the dug-out I climbed and in spite of my condition began tramping over the glaring sand-banks. To my surprise I found I was able to keep going very well, which leads me to the theory that the sun's rays give one a sort of nervous energy; had I been as ill as this in a temperate climate I'm certain I could scarcely have walked fifty yards.

On arrival at Raheng I found to my delight a white man in: not the teak-wallah who belonged there, but another who happened to be doing a cross-country journey. He was rather a pal of mine, and directly he saw me his jaw dropped.

" What's come over you? " he inquired.

" Had the gripes," I replied. " Got 'em still, for that matter, if I eat anything."

" What you want is an egg-flip. Boy! " he shouted.

Soon I was sitting in a comfortable long cane-chair, imbibing an enormous yellow concoction and feeling a good deal better now that I had a companion.

I sent off my telegrams, attended to the needs of my clerks, boatmen and servants, then settled down to enjoy the luxury of a decent bungalow and a yarn with the teak-wallah. At the end of forty-eight hours I was able to take to solids again, and we parted, he going north and I south.

The demon, knowing that every day was bringing me nearer to medical aid, left me completely alone for the whole of the boat journey down the Mae Ping, consequently I was able to neap along with the clerks. On reaching Paknampoh, however, I kept to my decision to go on down to Bangkok, for I knew it would only be a matter of time before another attack arrived worse than the last.

In Bangkok the doctor informed me that it looked as though I had appendicitis, but that as I was far too run down to stand the operation, I should go home.

My heart sank as I heard the news. I was out on a five-year chukker, to be followed by six months' leave and three-year chukkers thereafter. So far I had only completed three years out of the first five, and to have to go home now would therefore be breaking—and terminating—my contract. And, in spite of everything, I didn't *want* to go home. In a fit of depression I sought out the General Manager in his office and presented him with the doctor's report.

" I'll give you six months' special sick leave," said

the G.M. after reading it. "You've always done your work very well, Campbell, and we don't want to lose you."

Which was what I called really handsome of him.

Thus it came to pass that in a week's time I was travelling in a train down the Malay Peninsula bound for Penang, where I was to catch a B.I. boat up to Rangoon, the place at which I was to join the Bibby Line s.s. *Yorkshire*, the ship that was taking me home.

Penang is actually an island, with Georgetown as its capital, and a very pretty island it is. I didn't see much of it during my four days' stay there, for it rained continually, and when finally the B.I. steamed north one looked back in brilliant sunshine to see Penang and its mountain still shrouded in rainy mist.

In this B.I. was Beatrice Grimshaw, the novelist of the South Seas, who was also bound for England by the Henderson Line. She sat on deck most of the day with a companion, reading and writing, and the rest of us passengers felt rather awe-struck as we tip-toed past her chair.

At Rangoon we discovered there was a plague scare, so we all had to pass the port doctor before going ashore. In the case of us whites the inspection was purely nominal, the doctor merely looking at every tenth person and asking him how he was. One wag, who happened to be just in front of me in the queue, answered:

"Had a slight touch of plague yesterday, doctor, but I'm quite O.K. this morning."

"Ho, are you!" barked the doctor, all his kindly look vanishing at being fooled. "Stay behind!"

And stay behind he had to, nearly missing his ship thereby.

I had to wait twenty-four hours in Rangoon, and I put up at the Strand. Joe Constantine was sailing in the *Yorkshire* as far as Colombo for the sake of his health, and friends kept dropping in to wish him a good voyage.

The *Yorkshire* I found to be a very different ship from the s.s. *Blank*; after the *Blank* and the hardships of the jungle, both the accommodation and the food in her seeming the height of luxury. It was strange, too, meeting women, *white* women, of whom one had come to imagine there were hardly any in the world. At first I felt dreadfully shy, but after a week or so had thawed sufficiently to take part in the dancing.

There were a good many crocks on board, even amongst us younger fellows, and we soon broke up into the various cliques that are inevitable to sea travel. There were the super-burra-sahibs and mem-sahibs—ladies and gentlemen who played bridge from the time they left Rangoon till they arrived at Tilbury, pausing only now and then to tell each other of the iniquities of Gandhi. There were the athletic ones, always rushing about the deck and making generally a lot of noise (these, incidentally, being the biggest crocks of the lot, although they didn't know it, having to do this sort of thing all their lives to prevent themselves falling ill). There were the womanisers, preoccupied of eye and furtive of gait. There were the steady soaks who practically lived in the saloon, and there were the general nit-wits who flitted from one thing to another like bees amongst flowers. These latter played a few games of bridge or *vingt-et-un*, talked a little about the iniquities of Gandhi, took a little exercise, did a certain amount of drinking, and went in for a little mild flirting. But they never did anything for very long, as they always felt there was something better going on round the corner. I belonged to the nit-wits; there never *was* anything better round the corner, but all the same we enjoyed ourselves hugely: much more, I am sure, than the rest of the cliques put together. The stomach demon, though throwing out raiding parties, was making no real big offensives, and with the unpleasant prospect of hospital ahead of me, I was determined, bee-like, to sip honey while the sun shone.

At Colombo I and some others took a flying trip by car to Kandy and back, a distance of seventy-five miles each way, but all I can remember of the place is that the Queen's Hotel there gave us some really marvellous cocktails. Nuwara Eliya, which is a stage further on beyond Kandy, is, by the way, the one place you *must* know how to pronounce if you're to have any status out East; miserable creatures who pronounce it even remotely like it is spelt being spurned as trippers, or worse.

Arrived in England, after a consultation with the company's doctor, I was sent to a world-famous Harley Street specialist in tropical diseases. In exactly half an hour he had diagnosed me.

" You are suffering from chronic amœbic dysenteric colitis," said he. " And you also have chronic malaria," he added, as an afterthought.

" I see, doctor," I said, somewhat hazily. " Let's have that first bit all over again."

He repeated it: "And you must go into a nursing home at once."

So into one at Putney I went, there to be treated by the specialist with a course of emetine. Emetine, though the only real cure for long and obstinate dysentery, has a very depressing and lowering effect upon the patient, and what with having to swallow fifteen grains of quinine every day for the malaria, life wasn't too good. But I was glad at least to know that it was real dysentery, and not the after-effects of it, that had been troubling me all the time, and when finally I left the nursing home the specialist informed me it was lucky I returned to England when I did, otherwise in a few more months I would have been throwing up fungus in the jungles of far Siam.

Having passed the doctor as cured, I arranged with my firm for a passage back out East, then busied myself kitting up in London. Now that I knew the ropes I didn't waste money on thin pyjamas and straw hats, but bought some new gramophone records and a much-needed 12-bore shot-and-ball gun. I also bought an automatic pistol to replace the one stolen.

I went up to Cambridge for my last few days in England. My uncle was a Fellow at one of the colleges, and so it came to pass that I dined with the dons on the dais serene, and listened to long Latin graces of which I understood not one word, and enjoyed some excellent College port.

But at Cambridge I was restless. For me the place seemed haunted, haunted by those of my friends who had been killed in the War. And, whether I strolled along the Backs or in the town, those friends were with me continually.

There had been six of us, and as boys we had been wont to play truant on the rifle butts outside the town. We used often to get into mischief, and once, I remembered, an irate sergeant-major had taken our names and addresses and threatened to report us to the authorities. That had given us a scare indeed, and we had gathered together in conclave to discuss whether to mention the incident or not when we got back to our homes. And now, not so many years later, I was the only one left alive out of those six.

I shivered. A wet, autumnal wind was rising, and wet yellow leaves were beneath my feet; and suddenly I knew that I hated Cambridge and its cold loneliness, and a longing for Siam came over me. I forgot the horror and discomforts of the rains, and remembered only the still, bright dawns in the hot weather, the joy of camping in some cool bamboo glade of an evening, and the welcoming bark of little Sclave, whom I had left in charge of my boy. And so, when the hour came for the sailing of the P. & O. s.s. *Plassey*, the ship that was taking me back, I felt that I was going home instead of leaving it.

The *Plassey* was a small ship, carrying but few passengers, consequently there were but few cliques amongst us and we were quite a happy family. At Penang I left her, and found that again I was to have a stay in the island, for the Bangkok train did not leave for several days.

On this occasion it hardly rained at all, and, in the company of an excellent fellow from the Bangkok consulate, I was able to see something of Penang. We bathed at the swimming club, motored round the island, drank *stengahs* on the verandah of the sea-fringed E. & O. Hotel where we were staying, and one morning we climbed up the great 2,500-feet high Penang Hill named the Crag. I say "climbed," though we went up in bamboo stretchers carried by perspiring Chinese coolies as became the lords and masters of creation—this in marked contrast to my usual job of toiling up jungle hills on my own flat feet.

At the summit was the Crag Hotel, built bungalow-fashion and commanding a wonderful view. The sun was shining out of a cloudless blue, and we could see for miles. Far below the green slopes of the hill we had just ascended there shone the arm of water separating the island of Penang from the mainland; beyond the water the Malayan foot-hills rose gradually till they formed a great black ridge of forest-clad mountains stretching for league upon league to north and south, and cutting, as it were, the rest of the world completely off from us.

While we were waiting for tiffin in the dining-room, which was deserted save for ourselves, one of the numerous wild monkeys in the surrounding trees sidled through the open window and began jumping from table to table, snatching up the slices of bread already cut on the plates. My companion and I watched it, hardly daring to breathe lest we disturb it, and finally, after collecting up every bit of bread there was and clutching it to its breast with one hairy paw, it ambled lop-sidedly out of the window just as the Chinese boy entered the room by the door. One has heard a lot about Oriental imperturbability, but this Chink certainly didn't provide an illustration. He let out a howl of execration at the departing simia, at the same time treating us with a look that told us plainly what he thought of our conduct in letting the thief escape. But he got his own back on us when we sat down to the soup and demanded bread, by saying nonchalantly that it was all eaten!

And so at last to Bangkok. There I got a permit for my newly-acquired gun and pistol, and, after buying stores at Buan Suan Hli's, and being given a little red pup by one of our office-wallahs, a pup that cried mournfully for its mother when I took it away, I caught the train for the north, and soon the familiar jungle hills were around me.

Whereat I let out a sigh of happiness. I was home once more.

## CHAPTER TWELVE

# THE SHIKAR THAT DIDN'T WORK

My first job was to go to the Mae Tah forest to relieve another assistant, an ex-marine officer and, like myself, a member of the " Goat Club." The pleasant December weather had set in when I arrived there, and I found him in fine fettle at the prospect of enjoying the coming Christmas meeting in Nakon. I, too, was in good form, though for a very different reason; I'd had more than enough of doing nothing, and since the annual Nakon Christmas meetings had never particularly appealed to me—they savoured too much of " organised joy "—I was glad to be out of this one. Indeed, secretly I was hoping to get a great kick out of spending a Christmas all by myself.

The ex-marine and I, therefore, being in good humour with the world in general, fairly made the welkin ring o' nights in our jungle camps. It was necessary for us to do a round tour before I could " take over " from him, and there can hardly have been a patch of that Mae Tah forest that didn't ring with such songs as " If You were the Only Girl in the World," and " They Didn't Believe Me."

My companion was keen on putting in some practice on his pony with stick-and-ball in view of the Christmas polo, and he made a show of this every evening, the while I sat comfortably outside my tent and imbibed a " sun-downer." And the more I watched him, the more I impishly thanked my stars that I wasn't a horseman, and as such was expected by nobody to take part in the Nakon polo. (I once had a pony-race with another teak-wallah who rode as comparatively badly as I, at the conclusion of which a third teak-wallah said: " Well, I'm glad I didn't miss that. Always wanted to see the Aerial Derby, and now I have! ")

For that marine went through hell during those practices. He'd walk out of his tent in his riding-kit, a smiling, cheerful human being, only to return half an hour later, black of mien and brow, and muttering strange oaths about the uselessness of ponies in general; whereas all the time, as far as I could see, he and his pony had been getting on splendidly. But then, as a woman must suffer to be beautiful, so, I suppose, must a man suffer to be proficient at sport.

A day or two after he had gone, Sclave, together with Sunstar and the red, arrived from Nakon in the care of my pony-boy and my number two boy. I had been unable to pick them up on my way to the Mae Tah, and I hadn't seen them now for nine months. My eyes, however, were for no one but Sclave, and when I made out his little black-and-white body approaching through the trees, I signalled to the boy to loosen him, then gave my familiar call. Would he, or would he not, remember me?

His short, cut ears cocked. I whistled again. He looked quickly round him, saw me, and a second later his little body was streaking over the ground towards me. I bent down to greet him, and he was crying when he jumped right up into my arms; I swear he was crying, crying for sheer joy. The red pup I had brought up from Bangkok, which had increased in size with incredible rapidity, growled a little, and later, over their meal, there was a fight. The pup was the aggressor, rather naturally, since he thought Sclave was a new-comer, but he had to be taught and, after separating them, I gave him a good spanking. Thereafter the pair got on famously. I came to be very fond of the pup, but he was never the same to me as the other; for Sclave was my *dog*.

It is an extremely difficult thing to keep a dog in condition out East, and the casualties amongst those belonging to teak-wallahs were very high. I had luck, I suppose, in keeping my pair free from ailments (except when Sclave had one serious illness), but I also took a good deal of trouble with them. At the slightest sign of worms I starved them for forty-eight hours, then dosed them with worm powder, then starved them for another twenty-four—a treatment that was always efficacious. Mange and other skin diseases had always to be looked out for, and I kept a good sulphur ointment handy. Their diet was rice and chicken, made appetising with a little hot gravy, and the boy had orders always to show me the dish before he gave it them. I fed them twice a day, when I had my own tiffin and dinner. I have heard it said that chicken bones are very bad for dogs, as the splinters cut their insides; my two ate hundreds of chicken bones without the slightest harm. The worst ailment the red had while I had him was an extremely deep sore on the left buttock; maggots had got into it, and it was so painful that he wouldn't let me touch it. I solved the problem by tying his hind-legs with rope, then hoisting him up over a beam so that he hung in mid-air head downwards. While in this helpless position I gave him a good swabbing with iodine; he yelped and howled, for it must have hurt like fury, but the sore healed up almost immediately and he didn't have to have another go. Poor little pup; his end, as will be told in another chapter, was sad.

I soon found immense joy in my gun. I had brought out Nos. 4, 6 and 8 shot, together with about a hundred ball cartridges specially made for use with a 12-bore. These latter being only for big game, I generally loaded up with No. 6 while on the prowl. I bagged a good many green pigeon, a few snipe and an occasional jungle-fowl: nothing very much, because on the whole bird-life was not numerous in the hilly jungle tracts, but that didn't matter to me in the least; to stalk through the jungle, every sense alert as to what was going to turn up next, being to me the height of excitement. Compared to rough shooting, what pleasure there can be in aiming at driven birds is beyond me.

Christmas Eve arrived, and in order to celebrate Christmas Day I moved into the bungalow we had built on a knoll overlooking a little village on the banks of the Mae Tah. The bungalow, which was surrounded by a small compound containing stables, etc., served as a base for whoever happened to be in charge at the time, and after settling down in it I made plans for the morrow.

About three miles below the bungalow, on the left bank of the Mae Tah, there rose a huge and majestic crop of rock called Pa Lai. The face of the rock fell sheer down to the river, but the back of it dropped down in gradual slopes covered with thick jungle and honeycombed with caves. Only a week or two previously I had had occasion to climb up some of the rear slopes, and I had discovered a dark pool round which the tracks of pig and deer and goat were numerous; it looked as if bear and panther, too, must dwell in some of the caves, and I would celebrate the first Christmas Day on my own by organising a real, first-class, burra-sahib shikar (if so it should be termed). I would get, I decided, the whole of my own coolies, together with some men from the neighbouring village, to advance in open order across the lower slopes of Pa Lai and drive the game towards where I would be lying in wait. To this end I called for my head coolie and told him to bring the village headman along to me.

While I waited, my boy brought me my whisky and water. As I sipped it I pictured myself loading and reloading till the gun sizzled in my hands, the while bear and pig and goat and panther somersaulted and bit the dust all round me. By the time the village headman appeared I was considering the advisability of taking two elephants with me to carry back the bag.

" On the slopes behind Pa Lai," I said to the head-man, in the Lao language that I now prattled a good deal more constantly—though certainly not more correctly—than my own, " there are goat and pig. That is so? "

" It is so, master."

" Good. To-morrow thou, and as many of thy men as thou canst get, will come with me to Pa Lai, and there we will have a drive. Thou and I will wait at one end of the rocks, and thy men and my coolies will drive the beasts towards us so that we may shoot them. Thou dost understand? "

" Lord, I do not understand in the least," was the headman's simple answer.

This was a distinct jolt to my burra-sahib shikar idea, but after a moment's reflection it dawned on me that Siam was vastly different from India. In India jungle-men had been trained for generations to hunt wild animals, not merely for themselves, but for their white masters to shoot. Here, the Laos, knowing no ruling race, simply stalked animals on their own as and when they wanted to kill them, and a drive of any sort was therefore completely out of their experience. However, I wasn't going to be beaten, and called for my boy to join the two men standing in front of me.

The boy couldn't speak a word of English, but he tumbled to my Lao quicker than a strange native did, and so I often used him as a sort of interpreter when difficulties or unusual questions arose to be discussed. To him I put the proposition, but he also looked blank. I then rose from my chair, and to the accompaniment of a lot of *tang kwa*'s and *tang sai*'s and vague pointings towards distant Pa Lai, endeavoured to illustrate what I wanted done. At last, after a period in which the four of us, the coolie, village headman, boy and self all talked together, an understanding was arrived at (or so I thought), and the headman departed to spread the news through the village.

Pleasantly expectant, I rose early on Christmas morn, and I was just finishing breakfast when through the window I saw a sight that made me nearly drop

LOGS STRANDED IN THE HOT WEATHER.

my coffee-cup: advancing up the little knoll on which
the bungalow was built were the headman and about
thirty of his men, all armed with murderous-looking
muskets. If there was any shooting to be done, the
villagers weren't going to be left out of it, apparently.

I collected my own unarmed coolies, then, carrying
my shot-and-ball gun, joined the crowd.

" Lord," said the village headman, a pleased smile
on his countenance, " behold, we are here."

They were indeed, and I looked round in real
alarm. The primitive fire-arms, which were being
held at all angles by the men, two at least pointing
straight at my head, were obviously liable to go off
at any moment, and it struck me that the biggest
casualties of the day would be amongst the hunters.
Still, I couldn't very well have them disarmed, as I
hadn't made the point clear to the headman the
previous evening, so we would have to start off as we
were.

I led the way, followed by my coolies and with the
villagers in the rear. At any moment I expected to
hear an appalling explosion and to see on turning
round one of our number falling down decapitated,
but we got through unscathed and arrived at the
slopes behind Pa Lai. Here I was in a quandary;
obviously, the men with the guns couldn't and
mustn't take part in the drive, but I certainly didn't
want them anywhere near me. I finally sent my own
coolies off in a circular course with instructions to
work round and then drive straight down towards
me, after which I told the headman to send his men
off in the direction opposite to the one the coolies
were taking. What they were then to do I didn't

M

know or care, but they seemed quite pleased and vanished.

The headman and I were left in the silence of the rocky jungle. We lay down, with our guns at the ready beside us, and began the vigil. Presently, in the distance, I heard the shouts of my advancing coolies and knew that they had obeyed my orders correctly. Good! At any moment, I thought excitedly, some animal would burst through the jungle ahead and come right on top of us: a pig, a barking-deer, a sambhur, a panther, or even a *tiger*.

BANG!

I had been through the War. Whilst in the fore-top of H.M.S. *Prince George* during the Dardanelles operations, I had heard Turkish shells exploding on the decks beneath me; I had heard, too, the shattering detonations of our own twelve-inch guns, which gave forth such a blast that we in the top had had to keep our mouths wide open when we heard the Gunnery Lieutenant give the order to fire; but never had I heard such a truly awesome noise as that which now smashed the jungle silence into a thousand fragments.

When my head had stopped reeling and my senses cleared, I looked round, expecting to see the headman, whose weapon it was that had made the noise, stretched dead alongside me. But to my surprise he was on his feet, the smoking gun in his hand, bending over a rock a few yards away. I sprang up and joined him.

" *Meh*," he wailed, " it was a goat, master, a good, big goat. It came and stood on this very rock, listening to the cries of your Honour's coolies, and I fired at it."

He had indeed. "But where is the goat?" I asked, a question that was perfectly reasonable considering that the range must have been well-nigh point-blank.

"*Meh*," he wailed again, "I missed. See, here is where the bullet chipped the rock."

That finished me. Every living thing for miles around would have been scared away by the awful explosion of that gun, and in any case I wasn't going to risk it going off again in my ear. And to *think* of him having missed that goat!

"I am returning to the bungalow," I told him, somewhat shortly. "Tell the coolies when they reach thee that they can stay out as long as they like."

I marched back home alone, arriving there about one o'clock. By the time I'd had a drink, however, the humorous aspect of the affair struck me and I was able to laugh. I opened a tin of pâté de foie gras, a tin of Heinz tomato soup, a tin of Hunter's Handy Ham to accompany the inevitable chicken, and with the help of some Guinness and port made an excellent tiffin. I then played the gramophone, using the new records I'd brought out from England, and altogether had a most enjoyable Christmas Day. As for the men I'd left out at Pa Lai, they did not return till after dark, and a more crestfallen lot you never saw; they'd spent hour after hour in the gloomy jungle behind Pa Lai, now beating through it, now waiting, shivering with cold, for something to turn up, only to come back absolutely empty-handed. Thus ended my burra-sahib shikar.

In February I received orders to leave the Mae Tah

and to do the neap of the Mae Wang–Mae Ping from Nakon to Paknampoh for the third year in succession.

This neap carried ill-luck for me. The first time of doing it I had my cash-box stolen, the second time I nearly died, and now little Sclave was to have a very near shave.

This came about through my not being able to find a sand-bank, or even a shelf, to camp on one evening. We were in a very narrow and gloomy part of the Mae Wang river, with no village anywhere near and heavy jungle crowning either bank, and after passing bend after bend without a sign of a possible camping-place, I knew we would have to pitch tents on the top of one of the high and jungly banks. I had to cross the river twice before deciding which side to choose— both were pretty awful—and by the time my men had started hacking a clearing, it was practically pitch-dark and very cold. Sclave, who had got wet through swimming, was shivering, I noticed, and though I dried him as quickly as I could, the damage was done: in two or three days' time he had developed what I can only surmise was pneumonia.

There followed a rotten week for me, a week in which he never touched a morsel of food, not even the saucerful of beaten-up egg and condensed milk with which I tried to coax him. By day I caused him to lie under the bamboo shade of the big boat, and by night, when it was cold, he lay wrapped up in blankets beneath my camp-bed, the while I listened worriedly to his difficult breathing. At last he became so weak and thin that he had to be carried down to the boat in the mornings, and I was convinced his end was only a matter of hours.

On the eighth night after he was taken ill, I forced a wine-glass full of water containing twenty drops of chlorodyne down his throat, not that I had much hope of the medicine curing him, but it might relieve the pain in his congested lungs. Sure enough, his breathing that night was much quieter, and then, next morning, to my surprise and gratification he lapped up the whole of the egg-and-milk mixture my boy brought him.

Thereafter he never looked back, and, such are the amazingly recuperative powers of a dog, in less than a week no one could have told he had ever been unwell. His illness left me, though, with a vague sense of uneasiness; I was getting, I realised, a bit *too* fond of him.

Not far from the mouth of the Mae Wang I discovered a small lake which I am convinced no other white man has ever set eyes on. My big boat was sticking badly on some shallows, and to give it an opportunity of catching up my swifter and lighter dug-out, I stopped the latter and, gun in hand, climbed up the bank and proceeded a short way inland. I found flat, rather featureless country, devoid of teak or any other big forest trees, and presently came upon the lake, which was hidden by a circular wall of rushes and tall grass. Penetrating the wall, I saw that the surface of the lake was alive with duck, while snipe without number were feeding round the edge. Here was the sportsman's paradise I had so often dreamed of, and in a state of great excitement I rushed back to the dug-out to summon one of the paddlers to act as my retriever.

But, alas! though the two of us spent a good three

hours floundering about that lake, for the most part in it up to the waist, we never bagged a single bird. Every time we got anywhere near the duck, something startled them and they flew maddeningly just out of range.  In the end I managed to bring down a brace, but they fell into a morass which looked dangerous to penetrate.  I was so disgusted that I shot three or four of the filthy-looking water-crows that were jeering at me overhead, and the boatmen that night had a good feed, if I didn't.  At the mouth of the Mae Wang, however, I shot two brace of snipe, and my cook cooked them so deliciously that my mouth waters even now at the recollection of them.

On reaching Paknampoh I received a letter stating that my pony Sunstar, whom I had left at Nakon, had died of glanders in my absence.  He was nothing to me compared to Sclave, but he had been a fine pony and quite a " character," and I was very sorry to lose him.

Back in Nakon I found Swan in from our furthest forest and performing the duties of Forest Manager, the F.M. himself having just gone on long leave to England.

" Want you to stay in Nakon for the hot weather and help with the yearly accounts," Swan told me. " After that you're to go out and take charge of the Muang Ngow forest while Orwell goes home on leave."

This was unexpectedly good news to me.  To be in charge for eight months or so of our biggest forest while still a junior assistant would prove a most valuable experience.  I would have under me, for instance, about one hundred and eighty elephants, mahouts, coolies and chainmen without number, and all the villages in the one-thousand-square-mile area of the forest would give me fealty—all of which is rather high-sounding, but that is how I figured it out at the time, and I really wasn't very far wrong.

With this in prospect, I enjoyed my days in Nakon. With Swan I worked away in the office doing accounts in a temperature that rose every afternoon to over 100°, but the heat, being dry, wasn't so trying as might be imagined. In the evening those of the teak-wallahs who were in from their forests assembled in the club they had made for themselves, and played tennis and, after dark, bridge. (Yes, I *did* get some bridge in after all.)

Pleasant evenings, these were, with just enough men present to make good companionship without the hectic hubbub of a Christmas meeting. After tennis or squash we sat on the lawn in front of the club-house and enjoyed the brief gloaming. One by one stars winked out against the paling sky, and a few late birds flew screeching to their nests; around the club grounds tall lines of coconut palms, broken by pronged temples and the ghosts of native houses, stood quiet in the warm air; beyond them, beyond the great, yellow, heat-burnt Nakon plain, the purple outlines of the jungle-clad hills encircling the plain gradually faded into the night, taking with them, as it were, our brother teak-wallahs who were camped amongst them. The faint tinkle of buffalo bells, the clock, clock, clock perhaps of an elephant bell, the howling of a pariah, the laughter of a Lao maiden or the high, whining chant of some drover, then darkness. But not an English darkness: a darkness lit by the near and brilliant tropical stars and warmed with elusive scents.

On one such evening the wife of the missionary who had once bought Sunstar said to us all: " There's an Australian up here who's down on his luck, and staying in the town." (Had she been in India, she would have said " the native quarter." Being in Siam, and Nakon in particular, where the whites owned nothing more than a few scattered bungalows, she didn't.) " Like you all to help, if you could. He says he's an entertainer, and wants to give you a special performance in the club here to-morrow night. So I wondered if you'd care to pay to see it."

We naturally signified that we'd be only too pleased, and so, the following evening shortly after dark, about a dozen of us went upstairs to the little, hot club-room and, feeling slightly sheepish, paid our money and took our seats. The Australian, an almost painfully obsequious little man, withdrew behind a screen for a minute or two to get ready, and then the " performance " began.

It makes me go hot and cold to think of it. All he did was to clutch a dummy woman to his breast, and to the strains of a most frightful old gramophone dance round and round with her, now scolding her for some imaginary false step, now ogling her, now pretending to propose to her, and so on. The ghastly *feebleness* of the whole thing—and he'd been doing this before the Siamese and Laos, we presumed—made us wish the floor would collapse beneath us. He departed with profuse thanks for our patronage, leaving us feeling curiously depressed.

Which reminds me of a similar type of gentleman I

came across while rafting down at Paknampoh. Clad in a straw hat that would have disgraced a London cart-horse, a suit of whites that were only whites by name, and a pair of broken shoes, he appeared in our compound one morning and asked me for money. And I, mindful of the white man's prestige, and feeling very hot and bothered under the curious eyes of the compound coolies and raftsmen, gave him some in order to be rid of him. He then went on to my Danish friends' bungalow and asked for a revolver with which to protect himself while tramping through the jungle.

Incredibly, they gave him one. About a fortnight later the weapon was brought back to them by a Siamese official, who stated that it had been found on a jungle path by a passing (and superlatively honest) villager.

"But what has happened to the man we gave it to?" asked the Danes. "A white man, a poor white man."

The official didn't know; nobody knew. Nor, indeed, was that tramp ever heard of again. The jungle literally swallowed him.

When the hot weather was drawing to a close I left Nakon for Muang Ngow, taking with me the red pony and two new mounts I had bought in place of Sunstar. Though the company decreed that we need only possess two ponies, in my new and lofty estate I had decided that three were necessary.

In Muang Ngow I plunged into work with Orwell. At his desk in the right wing of the office we pored over maps and elephant registers and pay books and contractors' account books and rice and chili statements and timber measurement forms and neaping figures and Heaven knows how many other books and papers besides, and then, satisfied that, theoretically at any rate, I was possessed of sufficient knowledge to run the entire Muang Ngow forest, Orwell took the Nakon road on the first stage of his long journey back to England.

When he had gone I took over, with his permission, his comfortable bungalow with its comfortable furniture, sparkling cut glass and tasteful crockery, and when evening came I leant over the verandah rails to survey my domain.

Around me, hazed in heat, rolled for league upon league the huge forest that was mine, and as my eyes followed the misty contours of its swelling hills a great uplift came upon me. Was I not, for nine whole months, going to be a little King?

## CHAPTER THIRTEEN

# I BECOME A LITTLE KING

NEXT morning, feeling very king-like, I repaired to the office, to see a veritable crowd of courtiers in the shape of headmen, fierce-elephant mahouts and coolies awaiting audience of me. Seating myself at Orwell's desk, I commanded our Siamese clerk to let them in one by one.

"Lord," said the first, a headman, "I desire a rise in my pay."

It struck me as rather curious that he should want one the first day Orwell was absent, and I took up the notes that Orwell had left for my guidance. One or two employees were marked for rises, but certainly not this gentleman.

"That," I answered, "thou canst not have."

"Then do I desire to leave the service of the Great Company," said the headman, respectfully but firmly.

I hesitated for a second. I had yet to feel my way, to learn the ropes, and were I to begin by losing one whom I knew was the firm's best headman, it would be a bad start. Was the man bluffing, or wasn't he?

I took my decision. To give in would be arrant weakness. And what about that kingship of mine? I said: "Thou canst go to-morrow."

He salaamed and withdrew. The next was the head compound coolie.

" Lord," said he, " I wish for an increase in my wages."

" Impossible," I answered.

" Then I wish to go."

" Certainly," I replied without hesitation.

He departed. After him appeared a fierce-elephant mahout.

" Lord," said he, " it is time my wages grew."

" It is not yet time."

" In that case it is my wish to return to the home of my parents over the hills."

" May thy journey be safe and thy parents pleased to see thee," was my answer.

And so it went on the whole morning. By the time the tiffin hour had arrived, every single employee of any consequence had signified his decision to leave on the morrow as I would not grant him a rise. Since there was nothing else to be done, I walked over to Orwell's bungalow and sat down to lunch.

Though I had taken over Orwell's cook, an excellent Lao we had nicknamed the Prince, and the meal was therefore as good as one could get out in the wilds, I didn't enjoy it in the least, for inwardly I was confoundedly worried. Obviously, the men had put their heads together in order to get something out of the new master, who wouldn't know any better; but there *was* just a chance that they might carry out their threats to leave, in which case I myself would be absolutely done. You couldn't train a head coolie, much less an elephant headman, in a week or even a month, and with the whole of the work of the forest coming to a standstill I should be very properly in for the sack. On the other hand, to give in would prove equally fatal; the men would feel, I reflected, that they could do anything they liked with me, and directly Swan or the F.M. saw the rise in the pay-sheet, which would be enormous, again I would get into trouble.

After tiffin, instead of returning to the office, I remained in the bungalow, pretending to read a book but in reality just sweating, both mentally and physically. The men, I guessed, would be holding a palaver in the coolie lines, and I was wondering what the outcome would be.

After tea I strolled leisurely back. As I entered the office from the bungalow side, I saw with satisfaction that the whole pack of them were crouching in the porch at the other side, evidently in mind for an interview. I kept them waiting purposely for another half-hour, busying myself on some rice and chili accounts, then told the Siamese clerk that I would see the first.

The headman appeared and salaamed deeply: " Lord," said he, " I think that my pay is sufficient as it is. Wherefore do I not desire to leave the services of the Great Company."

" Very well," I answered, looking as though the matter was of very little interest to me one way or the other.

" Lord," said the head compound coolie, " my wages are all that I could wish for."

" Lord," said the fierce-elephant mahout, " my wages have grown enough. Wherefore shall the home of my parents across the hills not yet see me."

And so on down through the whole pack of those

brown children. By nightfall I had the satisfaction of having proved myself King.

.    .    .    .    .    .

I began a round tour of the forest. The hot weather still lasted, consequently very little work of import-ance was going on, but I wanted to get the geography of the whole of the open area well in my mind; I wanted to know the appearance and general character-istics of every side creek of the Mae Ngow river, so that when in the coming rains a " rise " was reported anywhere, I could at once visualise its appearance and know also the quickest way to get there; I wanted to know where every cart-road debouched on to the main and side rivers, this with a view to measuring and hammering new timber coming along; and, above all, I wanted to inspect the elephant rest-camps so that I would get acquainted with the condition of every elephant in our force.

The tour lasted me three weeks. The heat being intense, to save my carts and carrier coolies I travelled sometimes by night, and mighty romantic it was stealing through the silent, ghostly jungle by the light of flares. The elephants, tucked away in camps of twenty and thirty high up in cool, evergreen tracts of forest, I found for the most part in perfect condition, for Orwell was a man who took the greatest care of them.

One incident stands out. I was approaching a camp one evening, when I came upon a hobbled tusker of ours right in my path. I stopped dead, but the red pup, now almost fully grown, disregarded my warning and, instead of staying at my heels as Sclave was doing, went gaily on ahead. The tusker bubbled and swayed ominously as he watched the pup advancing (I have mentioned before how elephants instinctively dislike dogs), and then, quick as lightning, the great beast snatched up with his trunk a huge branch near him and hurled it straight at the pup. It missed him by a matter of inches—it was a mercy he wasn't killed—and the throwing of it provides a remarkable instance of an animal, other than a human being or a monkey, realising the use of a missile. For the benefit of the sceptical I should explain that by no stretch of the imagination could the incident be regarded in any other light; that tusker definitely took up and aimed that branch at that dog; I saw him do it at close quarters and I saw the expression in his tiny pig eyes.

The rains were breaking when I returned to the Muang Ngow compound to put in some office work, of which I found a surprising amount. On the second day back, in the afternoon, I was descending the steps of Orwell's bungalow in order to make for the office, when I heard a shout and saw, coming across the compound straight in my direction, a mad dog.

Now it so happened that during my recent stay in Nakon, no less than three teak-wallahs had had to go down to Bangkok for treatment in the Pasteur Institute there. The dogs that had bitten them had been only suspects, but such is the ghastliness of a death from hydrophobia that the men quite rightly weren't taking any risks and were going to have the whole treatment, a severe one entailing one injection a day for three weeks. And here, making for me, was no suspect, but a pariah in the throes of a first-class attack.

I can see that dog now, though I could only have stared at it for a few seconds. An ordinary yellow, flea-bitten hound of the village, the disease had invested it with a frightful sort of majesty; its eyes were both red and white, and they rolled; its lips were drawn back in a horrible snarl, and from its open, ravening jaws saliva drooled; it seemed to leave a trail of saliva behind it in the air; the tongue, red and flecked and swollen, lolled and jumped between the open jaws. It was the most horrifying Thing I have ever seen in my life.

Suddenly I galvanised into swift and frantic action. " I must get off the ground, get off the ground, get off the ground." With these words ringing in my brain, I made for the bungalow steps I had just left.

I plunged at them too quickly, slipped, felt my feet touch the ground again. The horrible Thing was on me, on me, on me. Out of the corner of my eye I fancied I could see the corner of another eye, a monstrous, rolling eye like the Hound of the Baskervilles', and terror lent strength to my legs so that this time I literally flew up the steps. Two bounds and I was on the table in the living-room.

The creature was tearing beneath the bungalow, which was built on tall posts according to custom; I *knew* it was beneath the bungalow. Jumping off the table, I rushed to where my gun-case was. Frantically I tore off the leather straps, flicked open the case, assembled the parts of the gun, slipped cartridges in both barrels, then rushed out on to the rear verandah.

My cook, who was there, pointed to a patch of

LOGS MOVING FREELY IN THE RAINS DOWN TO THE RAFTING STATION.

jungle beyond some paddy-fields behind the bungalow: "*Pun*," he said, "*pai pun leu.*"

A man, a Lao husbandman, was running out of the
jungle across the paddy-fields in a sideways direction,
a drawn knife in his hand.  As I watched him he
stopped, turned on his heel, faced the jungle he had
just quitted, raised the knife in a threatening gesture,
lowered it, turned again and began walking in our
direction.  All of which tiny playlet without words
told me that he had had as near a shave as I, and that
the dog had fled into the jungle, where it would shortly
die in fits.  I returned the gun to its usual place and
walked over to the office.

I had before now seen mad dogs being driven out
of villages by their sane brethren, the latter seeming
to know they were a menace to the community, but
then they had been in the first stages of the disease
and I comparatively safe on horseback, but this—
this was sheer horror, and gave me furiously to think.
And I thought about it still more when, a teak-wallah
of another firm happening along the next day, I put
him up in the spare bungalow and mentioned the
affair to him over dinner.

" Ever hear about X. and Y.? " he asked, when he
had heard about my experience.

X. was a tough old teak-wallah I had met once or
twice in Nakon, but Y. was unknown to me, and I
said as much.

" Y.," said my guest, " was a teak-wallah.  Same
seniority as X., and he died of—hydrophobia."

Shocked, I leant over the table towards the speaker.

" I'll tell you," he went on.  " Show happened
about twenty-five years ago, when X. and Y. were

N

both fresh out. They were going along a jungle path, apparently, with Y. a mile or two in front, when a monkey rushed out of the jungle and bit him. The monkey then disappeared, and Y., being a careful sort of fellow, bound up the bite with a handkerchief before going on."

My companion paused. The meal had been cleared away, and smoke from our cigarettes was rising lazily up in the still air of the room.

" Then along came X., a mile or two behind, and out dashed the monkey and bit *him*. Would have been laughable but for the appalling tragedy that followed. X., *not* being a careful fellow—you've met him, Campbell, so you know—didn't worry and, beyond thinking it must be a strange sort of monkey, did nothing. Simply marched along, in fact, without bandaging the wound till he came to the *pang* where he was going to stay the night. There he met Y., to discover to his surprise and Y.'s that they'd *both* been bitten, obviously by the same monkey. They then thought no more of the incident: after all, what's in the bite of a monkey? "

My guest paused again. Normally he was a jovial sort of man not given to serious talk. Now he looked very serious indeed. He went on:

" Several months passed, and then Y. started to feel ill, though he didn't know what was the matter with him. At last he went down to Bangkok to see a doctor, and the doctor couldn't diagnose him. He, Y., mentioned the bite of the monkey, but the place had healed up perfectly in the meantime, and according to the doctor, Y.'s symptoms didn't tally with septic poisoning. . . . Well, the doctor put him under observation, and after a few days they happened to meet in the Sports Club. There they ordered a couple of *stengahs*, and Y. was raising his when he suddenly put it down and said to the other: ' Extraordinary thing, doctor, but I . . . I don't feel that I can drink this.'

It was in that second the frightful suspicion came upon the doctor. It *might* be hydrophobia, so he took poor Y. out of the Club and summoned two other doctors. It was too late to treat him in the ordinary fashion, and they were debating what to do when the spasms started and . . . it's *said* the doctors killed him. Hydrophobia's a pretty frightful thing, you know."

My companion's story had ended. But I still had some questions to ask.

" You said that several months elapsed before Y. began to feel ill," I observed. " I'd always thought the symptoms came on much quicker than that."

" So they do as a rule, but exceptions occur, and Y. provided one. As a matter of fact, Beam the Consul told me he knew for a fact that a Chinaman had died raving only one day after being bitten by a mad dog, to go to the other extreme. Dog had got the Chink by the throat, apparently, and Beam's opinion is that the more severely you're bitten the quicker the symptoms arise."

I had one more question to put.

" X.," I said. " Is he still *waiting*? "

My companion shook his head: " No. X. *made* himself forget about it long ago, and he put his own escape down to the fact that he allowed through slackness his leg to bleed freely, thus letting the poison out. Y. tied his, you may remember. . . . Let's change the conversation, though. Had any . . ."

Thereafter we talked teak and elephants.

. . . . . .

The rains having broken, I brought my elephants out of their scattered rest-camps and, after consultation with the various headmen, put them to work. Some I placed along the banks of the Mae Ngow near treacherous, rock-strewn corners in readiness to break up stacks when a rise occurred; some I put to working logs down from the stump on the hilly side-creeks, and some to dragging in the upper portions of the creeks themselves. But always I had to study the ways of mind and body of each elephant, as pointed out in Chapter IX. I was like a general, planning the best method of disposing the different units under him.

A few of the elephants, before they could start on their duties, required re-branding. Branding was done, not by the old hot-iron method, but by an acid paste that sloughed the skin off practically painlessly, leaving the mark beneath. One had to be careful, while painting on the paste, that the strong, black hairs on the elephant's skin didn't flick back tiny blobs of paste into the eyes, and accordingly I always put on goggles when doing this. A new-comer would have thought it strange to see me, in topee and goggles, tracing a sign on the stern of some squatting pachyderm amidst a ring of half-naked onlookers. But we teak-wallahs had stranger jobs than that to do at times.

I had also to choose my personal baggage elephants. I would have liked to have taken Mae Doke and Mae

Nuan, the travellers always used by the absent F.M.,
and probably the fastest movers of any elephant, male
or female, in the world (I had seen the F.M. put them
through their paces across a clearing, and their stride
was unbelievable, while the longest march never
seemed to tire them). But—supposing dire mischance came to those peerless ones when they were
in my charge, what would the F.M. think on his
return from England? No! I left them comfortably resting, and chose two other cows instead.

I also singled out five *butchas*, aged on an average
six years and but recently broken in, and had small
howdahs supplied them with a view to their travelling
with me on my trips of forest inspection, and thus
gaining experience on the march.

Before I left on one of these rounds, young Smith
arrived from Nakon as my assistant. He was not a
complete novice, having done a year in other forests,
and, after detailing a couple of travelling elephants
and some carrier coolies for his use, I put him on to
inspecting exhausted areas. I then set out, taking
with me quite a circus: three ponies, two dogs, and
no less than seven elephants. It was very amusing
to watch the little *butchas*, with the tiniest howdahs
containing a pail or two on their backs, dashing along
behind the two big cows; they always looked afraid
that they were going to be left behind, consequently
the march for them was one continual rush from start
to finish, though I took care to see that they weren't
overstrained. Another teak-wallah I knew made the
practice of adding a cow of the bovine variety to his
retinue, this in order to get fresh milk on the march.
I drew the line at this, however, for not only would a

cow (bovine) considerably slow up one's trips, but it would tend to attract leopard and tiger to the camp.

My rounds while in charge of the Muang Ngow forest were of infinite variety and interest. I had to keep an eye on the main Mae Ngow river and the elephants stationed along it; I had to penetrate up the side-creeks and inspect working at the stump and the dragging in general; and I had to measure and hammer all the logs as they came forward prior to their being rolled down into the beds of the " floating " creeks.

The latter work was particularly tricky. Some logs, otherwise perfect, would have a nasty little curve in the middle; others would be plumb straight the whole way along but have a hollow running right through them; yet again others would be curly yet have a lot of meat on them; to classify each log in an instant under the waiting eyes of the hammering coolies was therefore no easy task, and, concentrate as one might, one was bound to make a few mistakes.

Every three weeks or so I returned to the Muang Ngow compound for a stay of two or three days in order to attend to correspondence and other routine office matters. And pleasant it was to have a nice dry bungalow for a little while instead of an ant-infested, dripping tent, especially as the rainy season grew more severe with the passing of the weeks.

About my second time in, I received a note from Smith stating that he was suffering from skin trouble and finding it difficult to work, so what ought he to do? There seemed no point in his lying up in a damp tent in the jungle, so I sent back a reply telling him to come in to the compound. On his arrival I found that the skin all round his knees was in a terrible condition; every day in the jungle brings one a multitude of scratches from thorns and the like, and Smith's skin was evidently very sensitive and liable to fester at the least little wound. I advised him to try one or two things out of his medicine-chest, helped him to bandage himself, then put him to odd jobs in the office.

The next afternoon we were both in the office when he called to me from his desk: "Come over here and look at me."

I did so. The bandages round his knees were wet through with suppuration, and the infection was spreading to his hands and arms.

"You're going in to Nakon at once," I said, for I was seriously alarmed. "I expect the missionary doctor will be there, and in any case you'll be near the railway head if it comes to going on down to Bangkok."

So off to Nakon he went on the morrow by the quickest means of transport I could devise, and well it was that I didn't tarry. For by the time he reached medical aid the skin was sloughing off all over him, and he was not only in torment but in deadly danger. He had to lie up in bandages under the care of the doctor for several weeks before he was able to return to Muang Ngow.

Smith's complaint was brought about purely by jungle poisoning, and it was while he was in Nakon that I contracted a most unpleasant complaint myself. I had been doing a good deal of wading through muddy creeks, and suddenly my right foot swelled up so badly that it was impossible to put it on to the ground; I rode back to the compound on a quiet pony, and after two days of lying up on a long cane chair, the foot burst between the big and second toes— I can express it in no other way. After that the pain and swelling speedily disappeared, and my boy said the trouble was caused by a tiny " meng," or bug, burrowing into the flesh and then breeding. Knowing the variety of pests the jungle was capable of producing, I believed him.

But I wasn't yet out of the wood. On my very next jungle trip I got shooting pains all over me. They continued till far into the night, and were only alleviated by my shouting to the boy and getting him to fill a couple of empty whisky bottles with hot water; these, wrapped in flannel, I had placed next to me, and immediately felt the benefit.

When I awoke in the sickly light of a pouring jungle morning, I had considerable difficulty in opening my eyes, for they felt as if weights were pressing on them. I noticed that my boy appeared somewhat startled when he brought the early morning tea, but it was nothing to the start I got when I looked into my shaving mirror. For I was gazing upon the face of another man: my cheeks were a brilliant strawberry red, and my face was positively bloated; even my forehead was so fat that it hung down in folds over my eyes, and altogether I have seldom seen a more unpleasant sight than this other man who was me.

How was I to treat him? I didn't know, for I didn't know what was the matter with him. I rested in my tent for a day or two, and the symptoms gradually disappeared, but they left me feeling depressed. The conviction was growing on me that I wouldn't be able to stand much longer the rigours of this jungle life: I was beginning to tire very easily for one thing, and a few more goes of illnesses like this last one would either send me home or else put an end to me; and I wanted to go home no more than I wanted to die.

A fortnight after the strawberry affair I discovered its cause through the arrival in Muang Ngow of a passing missionary doctor. He came on a night of wind and rain that will live long in my memory, and the way of it was this.

## CHAPTER FOURTEEN

## MUD AND A MISSIONARY DOCTOR

I HAD been in camp in the middle Mae Tang, measuring and hammering timber and inspecting generally, and, the work done, was riding back in the afternoon after the usual three weeks' absence from Muang Ngow. The weather had looked threatening when I struck camp, and I hadn't done more than a mile or so of the twelve-mile stretch when it began to rain and at the same time grow much darker.

A rough cart-track ran from the middle Mae Tang to the paddy-fields surrounding the Muang Ngow village. For a good deal of the way the track passed through very pleasant, open jungle, with green glades showing in the middle distance at the top of gently-sloping ground. Here, even in the height of the rains, the going was good and I was able to urge my pony, a white and a bit of a puller, forward at a gallop.

We reached the end of the open jungle and came to a strip of extremely tall forest that towered right up over the little track. The darkness deepened, the rain increased, and a great wind rose that set the tree-tops tossing and foaming. Bending low over the saddle, my eyes strained ahead for snags, I rode as fast as I dared through the roaring gloom. Behind me, similarly crouching, followed my pony-boy on the red.

The jungle flattened suddenly and the tall trees

vanished. We had come to the beginning of the paddy-fields, at this point rimmed by a ditch that was spanned by a slippery log. We dismounted and, crossing over by the log, somehow pulled our ponies through the ditch, then began leading them along the bunds between the tall and growing rice. That only a few months gone by we could have galloped right across these fields, seemed unbelievable.

Gradually the line of the village of Muang Ngow rose up through the murk. Arrived at the end of the last squelching bund, I remounted, trotted past the temple compound wall, whereon the red-mouthed dragons sprawled their uncouth lengths, and entered the village proper. A side street, a sharp turn right into the main street, and we were at the company compound gates.

A great surge of wind and rain met me as I rode into the compound. I thankfully threw the reins to my pony-boy and walked over to Orwell's bungalow. There I flung down my dripping helmet, dragged off my soaking riding-breeches and shirt, and descended to the luxury of a hot bath in the bath-room below. I then dressed and entered Orwell's living-room.

My transport I had sent in from the Mae Tang in the morning, and my boy had got everything ready against my arrival. Freshly-cleaned Lao silver bowls and ornaments winked in the light of the lamps just lit; on a round table was set a plate of salted almonds and a whisky decanter; a silver box of cigarettes was ready to hand. I sat down, lit a cigarette, poured myself out a tot of whisky, heard with satisfaction yet another furious gust of rain-laden wind roar round the bungalow.

My Siamese clerk eventuated out of the night, a tiny, inky chunk of the night itself:

" A good father has arrived.  A good doctor father, and craves shelter," he announced in Lao.

A missionary doctor!  I slipped on a pair of boots, flung a mackintosh across my shoulders, and, guided by a hurricane lantern, walked across the howling, rain-lashed compound.  Standing by the office, in the comparative shelter of the porch, was a group of strange carrier coolies, exhausted and mud-begrimed; beside them was the taller figure of a white man, also a stranger to me.

" I'm Campbell," I said, and held out my hand to the tall figure.

" Shaw," was the answer.

I had heard of Dr. Shaw, and a finer man by all accounts did not exist.  I gave directions for his coolies to be given food and shelter in our lines, then led the doctor into the light and luxury of Orwell's bungalow.

" Guess I can't come in here," he expostulated, with a rueful glance at his filthy clothing.

For answer I forced him into a chair and called for my boy.

" Take off the good father's boots," I told the Lao. " Then get a hot bath ready and put out some clean clothes.  Also tell the cook there'll be one more master to dinner."

My own glass of whisky was still half-full.  I took a second glass, poured out a tot, held it out to the doctor.

He shook his head, and I knew that he did so because of his calling.  He had, I now saw, iron-grey hair, a firm mouth, and wise, kindly eyes, at the moment clouded with fatigue.

" Where have you come from to-day? " I asked him.

" From Ta Nyong."

" No pony? "

" No."

Ta Nyong, twenty-five miles away down that awful Nakon road feet deep in mud. He'd marched that distance! I said:

" I'm the doctor now, and you the patient. This is the medicine I prescribe for over-fatigue," and again I pushed the glass upon him.

Still he was adamant, and I played my last card.

" You've just done, for some reason, a forced march into Nakon, and now you're on your way back to your mission station—also by a forced march. Worried about your patients, I suppose. That right? "

" You've got it," he agreed.

" Not much good if you get back to your patients a crock, is it? "

This time he drank the whisky, and some colour stole into his cheeks. My boy then announced the bath ready, and in half an hour's time Dr. Shaw had rejoined me, looking a different being.

" Now," I said, pushing towards him some sardine sandwiches the boy had prepared for us to toy with before dinner, " who, or what, was the cause of that march? "

" Inman."

Young Inman, fresh from Cambridge and with the roses of English air and English beef still in his cheeks! I'd met him once or twice in Nakon—he was a teak-wallah of another firm—and a decent fellow I'd found him. What had happened to *him*?

I asked as much. The reply was:

"Malaria on the brain."

I thought I had heard of most complaints since I had been in Siam, and sampled a good many, but malaria on the brain was a new one to me, and it sounded grim.

"Inman ran away from his camp into the jungle," Shaw went on. "Simply didn't know what he was doing, and if it hadn't been for his coolies rushing after him, things would have been all up. As it was they found him, sitting on a log and dangling his feet in a *hwe*. So one sat down on each side of him, while the others went off post-haste to get hold of Berry."

Berry, I knew, was Inman's immediate forest boss, and a great "character." He was a magnificent polo-player, had a little tooth-brush moustache, and looked the perfect "My-God-Sir-What-the-Hell-d'Ye-Mean?" type of cavalryman, instead of a teak-wallah. He was also a bundle of nerves.

"Berry got Inman into a bungalow," the doctor continued, "and sent for me. When I arrived, Berry was almost in a worse state than Inman with the worry of having to look after him. Inman, apparently, had had a severe go of fever before rushing off as he did, and I could come to no other conclusion than that it had affected his brain. So I took him into Nakon, and between you and me I'd have liked to have taken in Berry too. Man was in a terrible state of nerves, but he refused to come." The doctor paused. "Do you know," he added,

" I'm more worried about Berry than Inman. Latter 'll be all right if he leaves the country for good, but Berry . . ."

The doctor shrugged his shoulders significantly. And his words that night were strangely prophetic. Inman did leave the country and completely got over his trouble, but poor old " My-God-Sir " Berry died a few years later.

During dinner I mentioned my own trifling strawberry-face illness.

" What had you eaten that day or the day before? " was the prompt question.

" Curry, amongst other things," I answered vaguely.

" What odds and ends with it? "

I told the doctor. Coconut shredding, an odd nut or two, bamboo shoots possibly. . . .

" Thought so," he interrupted. " Plain case of poisoning. Something you'd had out of that lot just wouldn't fix in with your system. Don't blame your cook, though; might happen to anyone."

So I had been poisoned, which was yet one more example of the remarkable facilities this country provided for dying in it.

Thereafter we talked of the weather, and the news, and cabbages and elephants and kings. We also, for some reason, had a long discussion about sheep and cattle-driving as depicted in the novels of Zane Grey. At ten o'clock I took him across through the fierce and relentless rain to our spare bungalow where he was to sleep. I shook him warmly by the hand, and that was the last I ever saw of him. Though I was up early the following morning, he had already gone, gone up that awful road to his hospital in which, for a mere pittance and thousands of miles away from his homeland, he did what he conceived to be his duty. Truly a gallant man.

The terrific rain of the previous night had put the Mae Ngow in spate; the rise was not quite so big as I had hoped for, but timber was moving nicely and, mounted on a tusker, I spent all day riding up and down the river, superintending the work of the "ounging" elephants and seeing that they did not allow stacks to form. That evening found me several miles up-stream above the compound, so I camped at a place called Sup Oon, on the left bank of the Mae Ngow. Here Orwell had built a bamboo shanty to save the need for tents, and in this shanty I settled down for the night.

Before dropping off to sleep I noticed that my elephants seemed strangely uneasy. My timber-workers, plus my seven "travellers," were grazing, hobbled, in the jungle behind the shanty, and I could hear them trumpeting and rumbling and bellowing repeatedly; though most of them had probably moved more than a mile inland from the river whilst feeding, the sounds came to my ears clearly.

Presently I rose, slipped through the mosquito net, pulled on my mosquito boots, and walked out on to the verandah of the little shanty. It had ceased raining, and with a full moon riding above a layer of clouds, a dull sheen pervaded. On one side of me the Mae Ngow, now falling rapidly, babbled sooth-ingly; on the other, the black line of jungle rose, blacker than the night. What, I wondered, was going on within those grim depths?

RIVER TRAVEL, HOT WEATHER.

Two bull elephants sparring? Possibly, but that wouldn't alarm the others quite to such an extent. A fight to the death? *That* might be it, for in the past we had lost more than one good tusker in a desperate duel with another, and were this to happen again to-night I would be losing the services of a good elephant and the company the equivalent of five hundred pounds sterling. Yet how, in the dark, could I do anything to stop it? I asked myself anxiously.

There were the sounds again: a " pheeooaaoow," the short, stabbing blast of a frightened elephant, then the deep, uneasy rumble of another, then a succession of short, sharp blasts, like quick blasts on a steam whistle, the whole like ships in a fog at sea as heard from the shore. Hardly like a fight between two bulls, and yet, and yet . . .

Another sound came borne through the night, a sound that made me catch my breath sharply, a sound that was like a whining groan, starting on a low note, rising, then falling away in ghastly cadence. TIGER!

So that was it! A tiger, or tigers, were worrying my elephants, and my thoughts flew to my five little *butchas*. Too big to have the protection of mother and aunt, too small to be able to defend themselves after the manner of the tuskers, they might fall an easy prey. In a state of baffled fury at my own impotence, I stared through the dark till, the noise abating somewhat, I returned to my bed and fell into an uneasy sleep.

Early as I was up next morning, my elephant headman and mahouts had risen before me, and

o

when I hastened down the shanty steps I found the headman, together with a mahout whom I recognised as rider of one of my *butchas*, squatting on the grass awaiting me.

"Lord," said the headman, "the *butcha* Poo Noi was mauled last night by a tiger. His mahout here has just returned from seeing him, and from tracks on the ground it would seem that three tigers are about."

"Take me to Poo Noi," I told the pair.

Three-quarters of a mile walk through the jungle away from the river brought us to him. The poor little chap had some severe weals on his hind-legs, and his tail had been almost torn off close to the root. An examination of the earth near by revealed that there must indeed have been three tigers, a male, a female and a half-grown cub, and after consultation with the headman and the mahout I came to the conclusion that the parents must have been letting the cub practice killing on Poo Noi, for had they, the parents, attacked him, nothing could have saved him.

I gave directions for Poo Noi to be led carefully away from the district and then allowed to graze in a spot where good fodder was particularly plentiful; I also had a message sent to our elephant medicine-man, instructing him to treat the hurts with some of his numerous bark-medicines. This done, I returned to the shanty to have breakfast and make plans for getting my revenge on the tigers.

If I could find a suitable tree in a suitable clearing, not far from the spot where Poo Noi had been attacked, I would, I decided, have a *machan*, or plat-

form, built across a fork in the tree and then sit up
on it with my shot-and-ball gun over a live bait this
coming night. The chances were that the tigers
were still in the vicinity, and if I made the bait a
bullock, a creature that in marked contrast to a
buffalo was possessed of a terrific bellow, the tigers,
which I knew hunted more by sight and by sound
than by scent, would probably come on to the
scene.

Accordingly, after breakfast I went out again with
the headman, together with some of my coolies, and
soon we had found an ideal natural forest clearing,
with a tree overlooking it that was not too deeply
embedded in the rest of the jungle. The lowest fork
of the tree was rather far off the ground—eighteen
feet is out of reach of a tiger's spring and this was
nearly double that height—but it was on the safe
side and, after instructing the coolies to set about
building a *machan* at once, I went back to the shanty
with the headman.

There I told him to see about getting a bullock
for the night, but to my surprise he replied that this
was impossible. Impossible, I expostulated, when in
Siam bullocks could be miraculously conjured up
even in the depths of the wildest jungle?

" It is not that, master," he explained. " It is the
leading of the bullock up to the clearing that will
present the difficulty."

" Why? " I demanded.

" In this country there are two kinds of bullocks."

" I have only seen one," I said.

" They look alike, master, but they are not trained
alike. The bullocks for the carts are trained to be

led, but the others, the ones for food and the ones for the pack, can neither be led nor roped. And the ones here," he waved a vague hand round him, " are of the latter sort."

" Nonsense," I said briskly. " Can't rope a bullock? We'll soon see about that. Take me to one."

A minute's walk from the shanty brought us to four bullocks cropping the grass. I summoned those of my coolies who weren't engaged in building the *machan*, got hold of a length of rope, slipped a noose over one animal's head, and shouted to the men to pull.

Then the fun started. That bullock did a leap I had never before suspected any bullock to be capable of. Up went its hind-legs into the air, down went its head, and one after another the men, including myself, were catapulted into various bushes. We scrambled out, and there followed a show that would have done credit to any Western Rodeo. At last, by a good bit of generalship, I managed to get two ropes round the beast, with two different gangs of coolies hanging on to each, and when the bullock charged one gang the other gang pulled him back, and vice versa; this saved us from being chucked into the surrounding jungle again, but it was mighty hard work, and from the look of things we seemed to be tiring first. We were also not getting the creature an inch nearer its destination. At last reluctantly I had to confess that that headman had been right: there *were* two types of bullocks, and so, after releasing the specimen we had hold of, I cast around for another kind of animal.

" Goats," I said suddenly. " Let two goats be

brought." I had at first meant to say one, but as there were three tigers, one seemed rather short rations for them.

Sure enough, in about five minutes' time the headman magically produced a couple of black, hairy goats, and after giving the coolies instructions to lead them to the clearing in the late afternoon and tether them to a post, I climbed up the shanty steps for tiffin. As I was starting it, a young teak-wallah of another firm marched in.

" Just passing through on my way to Nakon, and heard you were here. How's things? " he asked.

" So, so," I replied, as nonchalantly as I could. " Just doing a bit of tiger strafing at the moment. Happens to be three of them round here."

My words had the effect I expected: he was newly out from home, and to be in close proximity to no less than three of these fearsome beasts nearly made the eyes pop out of his head with excitement.

" *Three?* " he exploded. " What . . . what are you going to do about it? "

I told him. " Care to sit up with me to-night? " I concluded.

" Would I not! And I've got a rifle with me," he exclaimed eagerly.

" Good," I said, with just sufficient nonchalance to make it clear to him that I, the old-timer, was so accustomed to tiger-shooting that the company of another man didn't matter to me in the least; whereas, truth to tell, I was mighty glad to have him, for that *machan* was going to be darned lonely.

After tiffin and a brief rest, we walked up to the clearing to inspect the coolies' work. The *machan*, a stout-looking affair of bamboo with a leaf covering, was already completed, so swiftly had the men worked, and we climbed up the bamboo ladder they had run up the tree-trunk in order to inspect our refuge at close quarters. There was just room for two lying down side by side, and as we were a good height off the ground I hoped that one of us wouldn't doze off during the night and fall overboard.

" If we can climb up that ladder," said my companion, as I was thinking about this, " why can't the tigers? "

Here was another somewhat unpleasant contingency to be faced, and though I was certain tigers could *not* scale ladders, I told him we would bring our pistols with us for repelling boarders, so to speak. We returned to the shanty, had tea, then, armed not only with shot-and-ball gun and rifle, but with a revolver and automatic pistol as well, set out for the vigil.

We were just out of sight of the shanty when I noticed that my companion was carrying, in addition to his fire-arms, a " wah-stick," or timber-measuring rod.

" What are you bringing that for? " I demanded.

He gaped at it as though it had stung him, then flushed crimson.

" Didn't know I'd got it," he confessed. " Truth is, I'm feeling a bit rattled."

And well he might have been, I reflected, for in the waning light the jungle was taking on a sinister tinge, and with *three* tigers about . . . my companion returned the rod and we hurried on.

Half-way to the clearing we met the coolies who had led out and tied the goats, and when we arrived at the tree the animals were unconcernedly cropping the grass. We climbed into the *machan*, and lay down flat on our stomachs, with our weapons all ready for use beside us. We had taken with us a bottle of whisky and a packet of sandwiches to fortify us as the night dragged on.

Our view over the clearing was excellent, and though it promised to be a cloudy night—we were in the middle of the rains—a full moon would be riding behind the clouds and I hoped it would produce sufficient light to aim by.

Dusk fell, short and eerie. I had spent hundreds of evenings in this selfsame jungle, but never before had I waited, in utter silence and with no native within a mile of me, in the expectation of seeing three slinking, striped forms appear at any moment. Of the four of us, the goats were by far the most phlegmatic; minus even a bleat, they continued munching at the grass.

Dark fell, and the goats ceased eating and placidly lay down to sleep. It was then I realised I'd made a fatal mistake in bringing two; had I brought only one, it would very quickly have felt lonely and bleated its head off, but it was too late now to rectify matters, and I could only hope the tigers possessed sufficient scent to smell them.

An hour passed, in which we gazed without relaxation at the faintly moon-shimmered clearing below us. The tension was beginning to slacken, when a sound came up to us from the ground at the base of our tree, and our nerves tautened rapidly. With beating hearts we peered through the tricky light, only to behold nothing unusual.

" Quiet," I hissed, for my companion had suddenly started to fidget.

" Those sandwiches," he whispered. " Where are they? "

" Eh? "

" Those sandwiches. Can't find 'em."

A horrible suspicion assailing me, I too began feeling around. There was no doubt about it: the sound we had heard was the thud of the falling packet of sandwiches, and it was up to one of us to descend the ladder and retrieve it. Strangely enough, neither of us appeared to be in the least bit hungry, though it was past our normal dinner hour, so we wrote off the sandwiches as a dead loss and broached the bottle of whisky.

Two more hours passed, and then it began to rain. As the clouds became thicker, so did the moon-glimmer diminish, and finally it grew so dark that we knew if the tigers did come we wouldn't be able to see them. We had, therefore, a little more whisky.

The rain increased to a steady downpour, which proved too much for our leaf shelter, and we got very wet. As mosquitoes were also feasting on our sodden bodies, we deemed it advisable to take precautions against malaria. We had, in consequence, yet another swig of whisky. The spirit, acting on empty interiors, went quickly to our heads, and abandoning the need for silence—was it not too dark anyhow to see the tigers?—we started to laugh and joke. We grew merry. We rained jokes down at the invisible, sleeping goats beneath us. We giggled and nudged one another. We told each other funny stories, very, very funny stories.

A new aspect of the situation struck us. The tigers had put us to a great deal of trouble, and now, owing to the rain, it was quite on the cards that they would arrive and devour the goats without coming to any harm themselves. Were we to provide free suppers for tigers? By all the gods we swore that we would not! We took some more whisky to put ourselves in good voice, then howled defiance at the tigers through the rain-whispering night. We dared them to come up and board us; *we'd* learn 'em if they tried! We also got wetter and wetter.

At last we tired and sank into profound slumber in twin pools of water on the floor of the *machan*. Thus ended the one and only bottle party that can ever have been held up a tree on a rainy night in an Eastern jungle, with three tigers as an audience. (For, as we discovered later, the tigers must have been extremely close to us at certain times during the night.)

Next morning we woke up, cramped and wet and shivering, and hastened back to the shanty at Sup Oon, to hear soon after our arrival there that the tigers had slain a water-buffalo not a quarter-of-a-mile away from our tree. I could not go on sitting up for the killers indefinitely, so, after sending all the smaller elephants out of the district—the bigger ones could very well take care of themselves—I returned to the Muang Ngow compound to put in some much-needed office work, the other teak-wallah going on to Nakon. Neither of us, incidentally, suffered any after-effects from the exposure, and we put this down to the whisky.

The end of the story is sad. Little Poo Noi, in

spite of all I could do for him, died a few weeks later from septic poisoning. The wounds themselves healed up to a certain extent, but he just got thinner and thinner and literally faded away. I had tins of kerosene sent out, and his body went up in smoke and flame.

During the three or four days I was in Muang Ngow after Sup Oon, I had my first experience of an earth tremor. I had just finished tiffin in Orwell's bungalow, and was rising from the table when I felt as if I were having a heart attack. For a second or two the world seemed to go round, and I went horribly dizzy. I sat down again, only to have immediately another attack a good deal worse than the first. This time, however, I noticed that all the hanging lamps in the bungalow were swinging to and fro, and, guessing at the truth, I called for my boy, who informed me in the most casual manner possible that the " earth had shaken." Considering that even this mild tremor was most unpleasant, I have often wondered what a real earthquake must be like. I shall never forget reading how, in the terrible Yoko-hama disaster in 1923, the earth rose up and advanced like a tidal wave, flinging aside everything upon it.

On my next trip out I had to inspect the head-waters of a side-creek of the Upper Mae Ngow into which I had never before penetrated, and on arriving at my destination I discovered a little lost world.

To begin with, the creek itself was unusual. Normally these creeks had a path of sorts winding along their banks for a good deal of the way up-stream, but this one was so steep and so full of sheer waterfalls that I had to climb, foot by foot, up the bed itself, and my baggage elephants had a terrible time getting along. Quite suddenly the creek came to an end in mid-air, and I found myself looking down into a huge forest basin, I standing on the rim. The basin must have been about seven miles across, and nowhere could I discern any pass, or break in the rim, connecting it with the outer world; consequently I knew that the headman in charge of the district must be having a difficult, almost impossible, task in extracting teak from it.

I camped on the rim, and next day plunged down into the depths to do some inspecting. At the bottom of the basin it was like being at the bottom of some nightmare sea; the light was green and sickly, as in an aquarium; the air was damply stifling, and the leeches fairly rained upon one. Mindful of how these pests had caused me to get laid up with mud-sores in the past, I got my work done as quickly as possible, then thankfully climbed out of the bowl. At the rim I took one last look at the queer, uneasy landscape below me—I probably fail to impress upon you how queer it all was; it resembled in a way some drawing done by a madman—then scrambled down the waterfalls of the creek outside till the comparatively light and wholesome Mae Ngow river swam oilily before me. This river I crossed, then day by day worked south, elephant inspecting, timber-measuring, and felling inspecting.

In due course I arrived at Fang Min, Fang Min consisting of one of our shanties set in a tiny compound on the steep, right bank of an important side-creek of the Mae Ngow. Here I had some timber-measuring to do, and it was with thankfulness that I settled down in the dry shanty after some sixteen days and nights in a dripping tent.

The first evening there I heard the clear, pure whistle of green pigeons in the jungle immediately behind the shanty, and accordingly I went out with my gun and a couple of coolies to act as retrievers. About a quarter of a mile inland I arrived at where, from their whistles, I knew the birds were perched; but pigeons are cunning fellows; they invariably select the tops of the highest trees, and since their light green plumage blends to perfection with the foliage, it is impossible for the sharpest eye to detect them. Gun in hand, I stared upwards, waiting for them to make a sudden flight to another tree, and thus give me the chance of firing into " the brown " before they disappeared again; but luck was against me, and when it was almost dark I walked back empty-handed with the coolies.

On reaching the little compound I heard one of the coolies say to the other: " *Meh*, but I am glad to be back again," and his pal warmly concurred. This striking me as curious, I asked the reason why, to receive the answer:

" Master, did you not hear the tigers that were roaring all round us while you were waiting for the birds? "

I certainly had not (if I had, I'd have returned home a good deal quicker than I'd left it, No. 6 shot being about as much use against tigers as a pea-shooter against an elephant), and I was still wondering whether the coolies hadn't imagined the whole thing, when an hour after dinner I heard the prowlers distinctly. They were much nearer to me than when I had listened to them at Sup Oon (if they *were* the same animals), and their moaning, blood-curdling whines chilled the night with fear.

I had had two of my ponies sent out from Muang Ngow that day, and they were stalled at one side of the compound. I walked over to them. They were plainly uneasy, stamping and snuffling, and my thoughts went from their danger to the danger my little travelling *butchas* were in in the jungle close by. There was nothing I could do, though, and as I hastened back to the shanty I was acutely aware of the powers of darkness against which no effort of man could be of any avail.

I spent an uneasy night, and was up at dawn, awaiting the reports of the mahouts. By seven o'clock every man had reported his elephant o.k., and I breathed freely. The tigers apparently had left the locality without making a kill, and we never heard of them again.

Work kept me another day at Fang Min, and that evening yet another excitement came along. I seemed, indeed, fated at this period to endure a succession of scares. About an hour before dark a mahout strolled up to me and informed me that his elephant, a huge bull timber-worker, had " gone fierce " and that he could do nothing with him.

" Is he on ' musth '? " I asked.

" No," was the answer. " Just gone fierce."

" Where is he? "

" Coming down the path now, master," the mahout replied.

This path ran along the right bank of the creek, only deviating from it in order to skirt round the

Fang Min compound, and very soon I heard the slow approach of a tusker from the north. My coolies, servants and what mahouts there were present bolted down the steep bank and made for the further side of the creek, and though I would have liked to follow their example, curiosity stayed my feet. What, I wondered, did a great tusker look like at close quarters in a first-class rage?

I was very quickly to find out. The sounds neared, then he appeared at the northern curve of the path where it turned away from the creek to skirt the compound. I was at the foot of the ladder leading up to the shanty in the middle of the compound, and should he choose to charge me I'd be in an awkward position. If I ran up into the shanty he'd knock the flimsy building down with the greatest of ease, while if I bolted too hastily down the steep bank I'd probably break my neck. I was beginning to doubt my wisdom in staying, when the wonder of him made me forget my danger for the time being.

I think it was his latent, slow-motion power that was so terribly impressive; the very jungle seemed to be aware of it and to shrink from him. And the hatred and rancour in his mien! On and on he came, very, very slowly, along the path skirting the compound, and then, when opposite me, he halted and swung his body and head from side to side as if seeking what to destroy.

Suddenly he froze. His tiny, glittering pig eyes had caught sight of me, and for several unforgettable seconds we stared at one another without moving.

I don't think I was conscious of fear; all I knew was that I had to concentrate in not moving a muscle, and finally, with a fonk of disgust, as though I were beneath his dignity, he turned away and, jabbing his tusks beneath a log by the path, hurled it through the flimsy fence surrounding the compound, smashing the fence to pieces.

The next thing to receive his attention was a growing tree. This resisted his efforts and sent him berserk. Bellowing and trumpeting and screaming, he bashed and lunged at the tree in an access of savagery that was positively sickening to behold. At last the tree fell, and, stalking on down the path, he vanished from sight, leaving behind him an impression of indescribable majesty and power.

When my coolies reappeared, looking somewhat sheepish, I sent several off post-haste by a circular route to warn a village two miles to the south of the danger, then again I spent a worried night; the fellow might turn out to be another Poo Kam Sen—and I wasn't Orwell.

To my surprise and relief, the mahout, a youngster, but a brave man if ever there was one, succeeded in leading him back from the neighbourhood of the village by the ear next morning, and I watched the pair go past Fang Min. The tusker was still in a rage, for he could only be induced to move forward step by step to the accompaniment of much coaxing, and I thanked my stars I wasn't his mahout.

Here let me pay tribute to those courageous Laos and Kamoos who are fierce-elephant riders. Every day they have to take their lives in their hands, lives that for the most part are none too congenial; for, as already stated, fierce elephants, being what they are, have to be employed in lonely tracts of jungle well out of the way of villages. The men's pay is, of course, higher than the pay of ordinary mahouts, and doubtless they come in for a lot of admiration from their dusky brothers and sisters and sweethearts and wives; but they certainly earn everything that comes their way.

Assured that no more danger threatened from the tusker, I mounted my white pony and galloped back to the comforts of Muang Ngow, with more items of interest than usual to be entered in my monthly diary.

## CHAPTER FIFTEEN

# THE BIRTHDAY THAT WAS GRIM

I CELEBRATED my thirtieth birthday by getting myself cut off in the sources of a very gloomy creek called the Mae Meeung, by going down with a bout of fever there, and by having my red dog taken by a panther.

The Mae Meeung was an important tributary of the Mae Ngow containing a lot of teak, and in its upper portion I found it almost as steep and rocky as the creek mentioned in the previous chapter. I put up my tent on the only bit of level ground for miles around, and a wretched site it was. Below me the dismal creek, which at this point resembled a narrow gorge, dripped and gurgled mournfully; around and behind the tent the dead green of the jungle walled up in a dense mass, the only splashes of live colour anywhere being provided by some enormous toadstools at least a foot high. These were of a brick-red colour, streaked with yellow, and gave off a most unpleasant odour. I ordered my coolies to hack them down with knives, but directly the toadstools were touched the stink became worse, and I had to leave them alone. Altogether, a grimmer spot could hardly be imagined. (It provided the background for my novel *This Animal is Dangerous*.)

The morning after I had settled down here, my birthday morning, I went out inspecting felling, and soon I was climbing hills that were steep even for

Siam; the teak grew on almost perpendicular slopes, and what with the rains, the ground was so slippery that climbing was a frightful job. Even my dogs were having difficulty in getting along.

Both the red pup, now full grown, and little Sclave invariably accompanied me on my trips and loved them. About every half-hour, while we were tramping through the jungle, the scent of some pig or barking-deer would send them off, yelping with excitement, on the trail. They never caught anything, and after about ten minutes they would break off the chase, follow back their own scent to where they had left me, then follow up my scent till they overtook me. I never attempted to stop them leaving my side, so thoroughly did they enjoy these runs, in spite of a lurking uneasiness I had that one fine day one of them might fall a victim to a panther, practically every teak-wallah in the country having lost a dog, either in this manner or through the panther actually sneaking into his tent at night.

On this birthday morning of mine I encountered a particularly heavy rain-storm; for some reason the rain also seemed particularly cold, and in a few minutes I was drenched through and shivering. I broke off inspection and returned to my gloomy camp, but by the time I had changed I knew I was in for a go of fever. Glancing out of the tent through the rain, I saw that the bed of the Mae Meeung was in high flood, and I knew, therefore, that for the time being we were completely cut off from the outside world. My transport couldn't cross over to the next creek owing to the steepness of the hills, it couldn't go down either bank of the Mae Meeung for the same reason, and were it to try the bed, the men would be swept off their feet by the rush of water. With this comforting knowledge I turned in.

At four o'clock my boy brought tea. The rain was still falling in a steady cataract, the sound of it on the canvas above my head resembling the muffled explosions of countless tiny bombs; mingled with the noise was the whining of mosquitoes and the thrumming of the spate in the Mae Meeung; on the ground-sheet the usual runs of ants were exploring for food.

I opened a tin of biscuits to go with the tea, not because I was hungry, but because I wanted something to do. When the dogs heard the crackling of the paper inside the tin they cocked their ears, and I tossed them some biscuits, being only too glad of their company. After tea I relapsed into a sort of vague coma, thinking, if I thought at all, about the singing of my quinine-sodden head and the pricking of the fever chills.

Just before dark, and it became dark before sunset in this gloomy gorge, my boy arrived with the lamp. It was then I noticed that the red dog was missing, and, assuming that in spite of the rain he had gone out for a nose round, I told the boy to call him in.

This produced no result, and a great disquietude assailed me. *Why* should the red be staying out so long in the rainy jungle just before dark when he might be in a comparatively safe and dry tent? I summoned the coolies, and soon I heard the " ugh, ugh, ugh " with which a Lao or Kamoo calls to an animal.

My boy reappeared, looking sombre: " Master," said he, " one of the coolies says he heard a cry in the jungle some time back. He thought nothing of it then, but now . . ."

So that *was* it. The red had gone out for a moment, only to be bagged by the sneaking panther that had probably been crouching for hours in the fringing jungle, watching the camp and waiting for its chance. I had been fond of the red, but were Sclave to be taken . . . Regardless of my fever, I jumped out of bed, threw something over my shoulders, assembled the parts of my gun, loaded both barrels, rushed out of the tent into the pouring rain, and stared at the grim and dripping jungle wall that seemed to mock me.

Somewhere inside it that foul brute was tearing to pieces the thing I had been fond of. I discharged my gun aimlessly into the jungle, reloaded, fired again and again. What good I imagined would come of it I do not know—possibly I thought the noise would scare the killer further away from the camp— but I suppose, what with the fever and the gloomy surroundings, I wasn't quite myself. Finally, I returned to the tent and collapsed into bed.

I spent a night of dreams, of sudden startings up, of fumbling below the bed to see if Sclave were still there, and next morning found me much the same and the creek still in flood. I had nothing to do and nothing to read, so I spent most of the day in sorrowfully musing on the red.

He had been a character, that dog, and his worst fault had been chasing buffaloes and bullocks whenever he came across them. I had never been able wholly to cure him of the habit in spite of beatings, and once he had nearly got both of us into trouble by chasing a bullock which had turned on him and tossed him into a bush. The bullock had then proceeded to gore him as he lay stuck helplessly on his back in a lot of prickles, and he would undoubtedly have been killed had I not arrived on the scene in time and beaten the bullock off with a stick; indeed, it was lucky the justly infuriated bovine did not turn on me. As for the buffs., the red was always trying their patience. And now he would never chase any kine any more.

I had been spared, however, the horror of having him taken right from beneath me. C., I remembered, had always made a practice of tying his dog by a chain to his camp-bed, and he had been awakened one night by a panther seizing the dog and getting mixed up in the chain and the legs of the bed. Picture the scene: the pitch-dark interior of the tent, the crying, dying dog, the fierce yet equally terrified panther clawing and snapping and snarling at what it must have imagined was a trap, and C. frantically endeavouring to get out through the mosquito net, to do he didn't quite know what under the circumstances. The end was that the panther freed itself and fled, but the dog was so badly mauled it had to be destroyed.

Then Orwell had lost a dog. He was in camp with a brother teak-wallah, and after dinner the dog went out and lay down between the two tents, which faced one another. It was a brilliant, moonlit night, but suddenly a cloud came over the moon, throwing the clearing into darkness. Orwell heard a yelp, and when the moon shone out again the clearing was empty; the crafty panther had seen, and taken, its chance.

That second night in the Upper Mae Meeung I feared for little Sclave as I had never feared for him before, and next day, my fever and the flood having abated, I thankfully quitted that gloomy creek for another and comparatively brighter one.

.     .     .     .     .     .

Young Smith, who had been completely cured of his skin trouble, had now been back in the Muang Ngow forest for some weeks, and on my next return to the compound I summoned him in for a rest— he'd been on the usual donkey jobs such as creek-clearing and the like—and for some company. On arrival he reported that he had just been sitting up over the remains of a buffalo slain by a tiger. The remains had been extremely "high," nearly asphyxiating him. It had rained relentlessly all night, his only companion had been a shivering Kamoo coolie, and he hadn't had any whisky with him, so his vigil had been considerably worse than mine. It goes without saying that the tiger hadn't turned up.

Smith recently had had a miraculous escape from death by cobra-bite. He was walking with the F.M. at the time, the latter being back from leave in England and out on one of his periodical jungle trips, and it was from the lips of the F.M. that I subsequently had vivid confirmation of the story.

"Smith and I were going along a cart-road," the F.M. told me, "when suddenly he let out an exclamation and leapt about four feet into the air. He was pretty pale as he came down, and we saw that a cobra was coiled in a rut in the road and had just struck at him, missing him obviously by a matter of inches. Extraordinary thing about it was that

Smith didn't know *why* he'd jumped; some frightful urge made him, he said, which was lucky."

On my second evening with Smith in the Muang Ngow compound, I thought he was looking unwell. In spite of his protests, for he was a very plucky fellow, I took his temperature. It was 103°, so I dosed him with quinine and aspirin and made him go to bed. Next morning he was no better, and that evening he rose to 104°. He was using the junior assistants' bungalow, which was at the opposite end of the compound to Orwell's, the office being in between the two, and as I walked to the office after seeing him I did a bit of hard thinking. Was it malaria after all? It might equally, as far as I knew, be half a dozen other illnesses.

On one of the office shelves was a medical book written specially for the use of men by themselves in the back of beyond, and, taking it down, I turned over the pages. Each illness looked more frightening than the last, each seemed to apply more or less to Smith's case, and the medicines prescribed for each were totally beyond the resources of any man who wasn't a chemist. I hurled the wretched book the length of the office, returned to Orwell's bungalow for a worried dinner, then sat up most of the night with my patient.

The following morning he was still 104°, when I had hoped the temperature might have dropped a little, and I realised he was seriously ill. I had now to face the difficult question as to whether I should take him into Nakon or not. Fifty-two miles of awful mud would have to be traversed, mostly in drizzling rain if not in a proper downpour, and I doubted

whether in his condition he would be able to stand the
discomforts of a jolting stretcher all the way; they
might kill him. Should I send for the missionary
doctor in Nakon? He might be out on a round tour
of the neighbouring villages, and in any case he could
not reach Muang Ngow within five or six days of
the messenger going for him.

It is difficult to express the awful load that settles
on one's shoulders when, alone, one has to decide on
the fate of a companion. The very man, whom in
other times of trouble one would be the first to take
into confidence, has now himself become the trouble,
and there is simply no one else to turn to. One is
alone, alone, alone—shockingly alone. My relief
can be judged, therefore, when who should appear
on the scene but the F.M., out from Nakon on a
trip to our farthest forest at Pohng. On hearing of
Smith's illness he immediately abandoned all idea of
completing the journey, and set himself to sharing
with me the task of looking after him.

That evening Smith was worse. His temperature
rose to just over 105°, and his body was like fire. To
cool him we wrapped him in damp sheets, which
reminded me uncomfortably of a shroud. There
was no ice, mind you, there were no jellies, no comforts of any kind. Instead, a grim little bedroom,
with the rain whispering on the roof, the lamp casting
distorted shadows on the bare, wooden walls, and
Death beating his wings trying to get in. I *knew*
Death was there.

We spent all night up with the sick man, and next
morning the F.M. was looking grave, while I was
convinced that Smith, who was not responding in

the least to any of the medicines we had given him, had only a few more hours to live. A liquid injection might help to reduce his temperature, but we had no means of giving it, and we now obviously dared not try to carry him into Nakon. We were debating what next to do, when a miracle occurred in the chance arrival in the village of a down-at-heel, half-caste gentleman who called himself a doctor. He could not possibly have ever taken any kind of medical degree, but he had the means of giving Smith the injection. He did this clad in filthy khaki breeches and shirt, and smoking a vile, black cigar, and Smith not only survived the cigar but his temperature actually dropped two or three degrees a few hours afterwards. We waited another couple of days to see that the rally wasn't merely temporary, then, since he was still very ill, the F.M. took him into Nakon on a stretcher.

At Nakon he was diagnosed as suffering from a severe bout of malaria, and though he recovered in due course, he was eventually invalided out of the country. I had the pleasure of opening the door of his car for him—he not knowing I was anywhere within miles of him—a few months ago in England, and can vouch for him being now none the worse for his misfortunes.

After Smith had left with the F.M. for Nakon, a weariness fell upon me, the weariness of nerves relaxing after hours and hours of continuous strain and worry, and for a couple of days I did nothing but lounge about in Orwell's bungalow. I read odd newspapers, and when these were finished sent over to the office for the Curiosity File.

The Curiosity File contained all the most amusing letters received by the F.M. or us assistants from natives who imagined they could write English, and since there was nothing intentionally humorous about the letters, they made the funniest reading imaginable. There was the Burmese, for instance, who wrote to the F.M. saying that he could not turn up for some appointment on account of a swelling in his neck about the " size of a polo-stick handle," which was a curious simile, to put it mildly. Then there was the unwittingly grim humour of a Shan contractor who reported that one of his coolies had been killed by lightning: " poor coolie, he go down to the river and he thunder-struck," ran the words. But these are only two instances out of dozens.

I myself had the pained surprise of seeing one of my own letters on the Curiosity File. It had been written by me to Orwell directly after I first came out some four years back, and it stated, amongst other things, that I didn't consider inspecting felling over awful hills " fit work for a European." As I re-read the missive, it hardly struck me as one worthy of attaining a place in the file, but then that only goes to prove how incapable an author is of judging his own work!

I also watched the peacock. This bird, a male with a beautiful fan-spread, was a pet of the compound, and though its wings had never been clipped and it could fly freely, it never ventured far abroad. It was a strange sensation to be sitting over a meal in the bungalow and to have the bird come sailing in over the verandah and perch alongside one. Poor creature! It was very proud of its finery, and one day it lost most of it through being mauled by a civet-cat that had had the temerity to make a nest for itself and its kittens beneath the boards of the office. We had heard a lot of squeaking and shuffling and scuffling there, but had put the noises down to mice!

When I went back to the office after the rest in Orwell's bungalow, I found an elephant headman in from the Upper Mae Tang with news that the baby elephant of one of the females in his charge had suddenly died. On my asking him what it had died of, he replied that he had no idea, and so, beyond noting the fact in the elephant register, I took no steps. Had it been a full-grown animal I would have made immediate investigations, but the babe, which had been only a few months old, had probably died of some babyish complaint that wouldn't spread to the other elephants in the camp.

That evening the same headman, whom incidentally I had never trusted very much, returned to me with a request for medicine, saying he had *chep tawng*, or the stomach-ache. I gave him the usual castor-oil, and my surprise can be imagined when the following morning he reappeared with the whole of his mahouts and chainmen, all in from the Mae Tang and all suffering from *chep tawng*. My surprise, however, soon gave way to indignation when I tumbled to the fact that obviously they had devoured the dead baby elephant, to be rewarded with first-class attacks of colic.

I don't quite know why, but this realisation made me furiously angry. I suppose it is no worse to eat baby elephant than it is to eat veal, but we dealt with elephants so much, and thought of them so highly, that the act seemed almost to savour of cannibalism. It was also on the cards that the men had slain the little creature on purpose to eat it, but I could obtain no proof; in response to my query as to where the body was, the headman had informed me he had burnt it according to custom, so, beyond giving the men such strong doses of castor-oil that they would remember the incident for a very long time, again I could do nothing.

The office work clewed up, including the settling of an account from the half-caste " doctor " for attendance on Smith, the " doctor " signing himself as " Physician and Surgeon, Muang Ngow," I went back to the jungle for another round. On this occasion a great depression descended on me as the roofs of the village faded into the rainy distance. I felt listless and run down, and was more than ever convinced that I could not much longer stand out against the hardships and fatigue inevitable to a teak-wallah's life. I would stick it out, though, as long as I could, I decided.

Why did I make this decision?

Because I loved the life.

Why did I love it?

That was harder to answer. Surely I had every cause to hate it?

## CHAPTER SIXTEEN

# LAUGHTER ON THE MAE YOME

At last that seemingly interminable rainy season drew to a close, and mighty glad I was when it did. Quite apart from leeches, fever and a thousand other ailments and discomforts, it would be nice to get a decent smoke again; in the rains cigarettes became so limp that they would scarcely draw.

After a few weeks spent in neaping the drying-up side-creeks of the Mae Ngow, I neaped the Mae Ngow itself down to its mouth where it ran into the Mae Yome. This I did on foot without boats, and in some parts of the lower Mae Ngow I had considerable difficulty in getting along; here, for long stretches, the river became a succession of deep pools linked by thin runs of water: these pools were fringed by elephant-grass twice the height of a man, and to get at the various batches of logs resting in them was a fearful job. One would hack one's way through the grass, coughing and spluttering out drifts of flying " down," then, reaching the water's edge, peer round the pool; if there were no logs there, one would go back through the grass, then on down the river to the next pool; if there were any there, you tried to make out how many (a difficult task when several were nestling together side by side), and in the end you either guessed the number and classifications, or

237

else you resignedly plunged into the water and swam over to the timber, holding your notebook up with one hand and paddling with the other. Curiously enough, getting immersed in river-water never brought on fever, though a drenching in rain-water often had that effect; I suppose the reason is that the former was very much warmer.

At the mouth of the Mae Ngow I camped in a clearing on the corner of land between the two rivers. Here I worked on neap figures. I had Orwell's neap figures for the previous year with me, also a record of the numbers of new logs placed in the Mae Ngow during the present year. By adding these two together, then subtracting my own new neap figures, I arrived at the number of logs that must have floated out into the main Mae Yome in the rains just over. From the rises that had taken place during the rains, I had already made a rough estimate, and it was interesting to see that out of a total of several thousand logs my guess had only been a few hundred out.

This particular camp was in a lovely spot. Below me on the right the Mae Ngow, in marked contrast to the deep pools a little higher up, ran shallow and clear and steely-white over a clean gravel bed into the Mae Yome. In front of me, vanishing from sight to right and left round jungle-clad promontories, flowed the mighty parent river, which still ran broad and deep and yellow from the recent rains. On the opposite bank of the Mae Yome the main watershed rose in a succession of forest-clad terraces that terminated in the bright blue of a cloudless sky. Out of sight, some few bends higher up the Mae Yome, the murmur of the mighty Keng Sua Ten rapids lulled the brooding silence of the eternal hills.

While camped here, some mail coolies drifted out from the Muang Ngow compound with letters from home and Nakon. Amongst the latter was a note from the F.M. telling me to do the neap of the main Mae Yome from the mouth of the Mae Ngow down to a place called Prae. If I couldn't obtain boats, he said, I was to use bamboo rafts.

I read the instructions with delight. By sheer chance I was at the very starting-place, the length of the journey—some sixty miles—was just right for interest without boredom, and I had never been along this particular stretch of the Mae Yome before. I sent my coolies off looking for fishermen from whom to hire boats, and though they found a small dug-out for my personal use, no large boat for kit and servants was procurable. Accordingly I put the men on to building a bamboo raft, which when ready was loaded up with my tents and camp furniture. The baggage elephants were sent back to rest near Muang Ngow till I returned from Prae, and all was ready for the neap.

The night before we started heavy rain fell, the clouds coming from the north-east. (There is a brief N.E. monsoon which succeeds the much longer and wetter S.W.) When morning broke it had stopped raining, but there was quite a rise in the Mae Yome. Only an odd log or two was moving, however, as ninety-nine per cent. of the timber had been stacked high by the previous floods, and, confident that my neap wouldn't be interfered with, we pushed off.

The start was made in grand style. The current

was very swift, there were no waterfalls ahead of us to make me fear for the raft, and as very little timber was encountered, we had practically no delays and swept on mile after mile down the broad and glorious river. Soon I was singing from pure happiness, and the paddlers in my dug-out were exchanging jokes with the coolies, polemen and servants on the raft keeping station behind. We waved to the pretty, dark-haired Lao girls in the occasional villages we passed, we waved to the monkeys up the trees, we waved to the stupid water-buffaloes. Life was fun.

This sort of thing went on for two whole days, and then, on the third, Nemesis overtook us with startling suddenness. More rain must have fallen overnight round the distant sources of the Mae Yome, for on the third morning the power of the river had increased in spite of cloudless blue skies. We went off faster than ever, and about eleven o'clock came to a sharp bend, round which the current tore at tremendous speed under a high, overhanging bank. We in the dug-out ahead rounded the bend safely, but nearly came to grief on the branch of a submerged tree that was sticking up right in our course. The dug-out missed the branch by inches, and I shouted a warning to the cumbersome raft following. The polemen saw the danger, but the water was too deep for the poles to bite properly, and the raft went plumb on to the snag. For a moment it stayed put, as though dumb-founded at having its course thus arrested; then, as the current surged over it, it rose up in a most uncanny manner and turned completely over, shedding ser-vants, coolies, tents, polemen, furniture, lamps and so on in all directions into the river.

THE REST BY THE TEMPLE.

The Prince, my majestic cook borrowed from Orwell, hardly lived up to his nickname as he fairly shot off the capsizing raft and began to make frantic strokes towards the safety of the opposite bank, which was low-lying and out of the path of the fierce current. Luckily all the men could swim, or there would have been a tragedy, and I and the paddlers in the dug-out started salvaging all the stuff that hadn't sunk as it floated down to us. This we carried or towed over to the flat bank, then I scrambled out of the dug-out in order to take stock of my losses.

Before starting, I noticed that the men were casting sheepish, half-frightened glances in my direction, evidently thinking that shortly I would vent my temper on some of them for allowing the accident to happen. It had been unavoidable, however, and the humour of the situation striking me, I sat down on the bank and laughed till my sides ached.

Presently a coolie began to laugh, then a paddler, then my boy, and soon all my men were laughing too. Goodness, how we laughed, sitting there by the ruins of the kit that October morn on the bank of the amber Mae Yome! They were good fellows, those Laos and Kamoos, obedient and willing, and ready to see the bright side of anything provided you did. The one thing they did not understand was sarcasm, that being completely beyond them; what you said they took quite literally—and why not?

By great good fortune I'd had the sense to keep my two most valuable possessions, my gun and my cash-box, with me in the dug-out, none the less my losses were serious. The tents and camp furniture had, of course, floated, but the whole of my lamps,

Q

cooking utensils, crockery, plate, and tinned and bottled foods had gone to the bottom for a start. It was impossible to recover a single item in view of the depth of the water and the swiftness of the current, so, after drying the articles saved, we turned the raft the right way up and pushed on as fast as we could in the hopes of reaching a village before dark.

In this we were successful. We camped on a sand-bar near a village, and while my men rushed up to explore the market-place, if one existed, I watched a Siamese who was probably a minor Government official making camp on the bank opposite to me. He had two tiny Siamese ponies with him, a few servants and a tiny tent, and as his camp fire winked out through the night my heart warmed to him; we were travellers sharing a common lot.

That night, in spite of the pot-and-pan shortage and other factors, my dinner tasted exactly the same as ever, and I got along with a knife of sorts obtained from the village, and an impromptu bamboo fork. What *did* worry me was the loss of the sugar and the lamps. The former was irreplaceable, but sub-stitutes for the latter were provided by my boy filling the tops of some cigarette tins with pigs' fat and placing short lengths of string in them to act as wicks; the result was only a glimmer, but it was better than nothing.

In this fashion I made the rest of the neap to Prae. I returned to Nakon from there by train, made out a claim on the company for the loss of part of my kit in their service, a claim that they met in full, then continued on back to Muang Ngow by the usual road. Here I spent my remaining weeks in charge of the forest getting everything ready for Orwell's return, then at Christmas time went in to Nakon again in order to take part in the teak-wallahs' annual meeting.

These meetings were rather hectic affairs, and this one proved no exception. Your time was occupied from the time you got up in the morning till you went to bed the following morning. About ten o'clock you would rush down to the club to play off some competition round of tennis or golf or squash; at twelve you would have to help mark off the ground for the coming teak-wallahs' gymkhana, and at twelve-thirty it would be a scamper to arrive at So-and-So's bungalow to fulfil a promise to have short drinks with him. Then another scamper back to lunch, a brief sleep in the afternoon, a bleary cup of tea, and a second rush to the club for more competitive games. Whiskies-and-sodas at dark, followed by a dash back to your bungalow for a bath and change before going out to dine somewhere. After dinner you would troop round with several others to where someone was throwing a party, and there would be singing and general fooling around till three or four o'clock in the morning. Six hours later you would be up to start the round all over again.

This sort of routine was all very well for a day or two, but a solid fortnight of it was a bit too much even for the toughest heads and hearts. Towards the end of a meeting strong men began to wilt visibly at the knees, and I'm sure most of us were dying to get out into the jungle again in order to have a nice rest doing some work. The meetings, however, were good in that they gave lonely men the companionship they needed, if only for a little time.

At the beginning of January I returned with Orwell to Muang Ngow, and having handed the forest over to him, I became once more his assistant. I hadn't resumed my normal duties more than a fortnight when the stomach demon suddenly resurrected itself and attacked me. This time, however, I was taking no chances; I went at once into Nakon, then on to Chiengmai, where there lived a missionary doctor of great repute. He listened to my case, examined me, and his verdict was what I expected.

' You've got no fresh infection," he said. " But the fact is you'll never really be fit until you've done a good two years in a temperate climate. And that means . . ." he hesitated.

" Chucking the job and going home for good," I finished for him.

He nodded. " Sorry? " he asked kindly.

" Fairly," I answered non-committally, then, armed with his report, I returned to Nakon.

There followed telegrams between the F.M. and the G.M. in Bangkok, from which it transpired that, the rush season being on, there was no berth available for me till the Royal Dutch mail steamer *Königin den Nederlanden* sailed from Singapore at the beginning of April. I had therefore over two months to wait.

" There's nothing for you to do here, Campbell," said the F.M. " But there's some girdling wants inspecting in Swan's forest. Think you can manage it? "

I was only too pleased to reply in the affirmative. The stomach demon was quiescent again, and to have a chance properly of seeing our farthest forest, close by the borders of Indo-China and the banks of the mighty Mae Kong, was not one to be missed. I should also be able to inspect at close quarters the locality at one time terrorised by the famous man-eater of Muang Pohng.

And so it came to pass that I set out on my last, and what turned out to be my grimmest, jungle adventure.

## CHAPTER SEVENTEEN

# BENIGHTED

I TOOK the road for the north, passed duly through Muang Ngow, and held on my northerly course. At Prayow I swung sharp right and struck an apology of a road heading north-east; for mile upon mile it rose and dipped through heat-hazed, monotonous jungle, though at nights it was so cold that one shivered. Eventually I struck a huge plain, covered partly with paddy-field stubble, across which I rode, slowly so as not to get too far ahead of the guides I had hired and the bullock-carts carrying my kit.

Presently, ahead of me, there rose up a purple line of very high hills. Under their shadow, in a little shanty I knew must have been run up by Swan, for I was now on the outskirts of his forest, I spent my seventh night after leaving Nakon. Next day we pierced the line of the hills by following a road so rough that I feared for my groaning carts. On the other side of the hills we emerged into a type of country I had never before beheld in Siam: flat teak forest.

One of our assistants—the man I was going to relieve—was in camp in this flat forest, and with the help of guides I found him. In order to show me the ropes he spent two days with me, and as I tramped round with him I thought I had never seen more depressing country. Although the hot weather, my favourite season, was beginning, I could experience no thrill in the spectacle of thousands upon thousands of trees towering silently up to the brassy skies; in the Mae Ngow forest they had presented a grand and austere beauty; here they were just grim and silent and forbidding. The creeks, instead of tumbling down hills, with many a waterfall and pool and twist and turn to give them interest, resembled man-made cuttings through the flat earth. They reminded one, indeed, of what the road looks like at home when the workmen are getting at the gas or drains. At this time of the year they were naturally dry, but grass and other debris wrapped round the base of trees along the edges told me that they could rise high enough in the rains.

Near our camp was a *hai*. A *hai* is a little clearing in the forest made by a Lao husbandman who wishes to grow tobacco and cotton, or maize, pumpkins and the like; when it is ready he builds a *pang*, or rough bamboo shanty, for himself and his family, and in it he lives, often at a considerable distance away from his village, until he has grown enough commodities to pay off his annual head tax and buy some clothing. Normally these *hais* were cheerful little places to come upon during the march; guarded on all sides by criss-cross bamboo anti-devil signs, and often possessing a little bamboo shrine in which were set pathetic offerings of rice, cakes and candles to the glory of the Lord Gautama, they made convenient halting-places for a rest and a chat with the wife of the husbandman and her sloe-eyed piccaninnies. This *hai*, however, was a grim affair. The initial work of clearing had been badly done, so that it was rank with weeds and littered with snags, the *pang* had been erected in a most slovenly manner, while the inhabitants were sour-looking creatures who would have turned my condensed milk had they glanced at it.

Altogether a depressing locality, and one made more so by the fact that the mosquitoes, instead of being the ordinary " tiger " variety, were the little brown malaria-bringing anopheles. What the place must be like in the rains I could not imagine, and I asked my companion, who had done several seasons here.

" What's it like? " He gave the proverbial short, mocking laugh. " Snipe-marsh isn't in it, *I* can tell you. Being so flat, country's flooded for miles around, so you're never out of water. You camp in water. You walk in water the whole time you're inspecting. You sit down in water to eat. You sleep in water. And if I'd got any brains I'd have had water on the brain too. Yes. Long ago."

" Mud-sores? " I queried.

Again that laugh, shorter and yet more mocking. " *You* don't know what mud-sores are," he complained. " Muang Ngow? Nonsense! Things you get there are nothing. But here . . ." he paused and sucked at a pipe that looked as if it, too, had suffered from the general depression, " here you get great holes in your legs, and you have to go down to Bangkok to have them filled in. I know, for I've had 'em."

In at least the last part of his statement I knew he was not exaggerating, for he must have worked in indescribable conditions. And I remembered the F.M. telling me how, when he had been in the district, he had often awakened in the morning with the sheets covered with blood, leeches having actually looped up into his bed!!

When my companion left, he took with him my ponies, for it had been arranged that on my return trip I was to strike across to the Upper Mae Yome and neap down that river to Keng Sua Ten, thence going to Muang Ngow, where I would pick up the ponies again and go on to Nakon by road.

I began girdling inspection, and never have I known such monotonous work. One part of the forest was exactly like another, and in spite of nearly five years' jungle experience behind me, I was always on the verge of getting lost. A compass would have been useful, but the F.M., who several months ago had indented on Head Office for some, had received to his combined annoyance and amusement a parcel of *geometrical* compasses in return.

The only interesting features of this flat forest were signs of a bygone civilisation. Ruins of temples, sometimes with only the tip of a pagoda showing above masses of rubble and brick and stone, which in turn were covered with vines and creeper, showed here and there, while in places the ground looked as if ages and ages ago, before the forest had grown over it, paddy-fields had existed.

Soon, owing to the presence of the little anopheles, I began to go down with mild bouts of " low fever." I would wake up feeling well enough, but exactly at noon the fever would start and last till ten o'clock at night. This went on for a good many days with most amazing regularity; I could quite literally tell the time by the onset of the attacks. I kept on working to begin with, then finally gave up in disgust and confined myself to the tent.

It was grim.   Mails were few and far between, so I had nothing to read, and owing to the leafless state of the forest practically no shade existed, and by day the heat in the tent was terrific.   For hour after hour I sat and stewed, listening to the maddening shrill of the cicalas perched in millions on the heat-whitened trees, and watching the shadow of the tent gradually lengthen as the sun strolled over the brassy skies.

The fever passed off, and after a little more inspecting girdling it was time for me to go into Pohng in order to start the neap, which would be the first stage of my long journey back to far-away England.

A two-days' march brought me out of the flat country to where the little railway Swan had built ran through hilly forest.   This railway was a magnificent achievement.   When first the forest hereabouts had been inspected for possible teak extraction (this several years before I came out), it was found that the only river anywhere near the growing teak had the bad taste to run into the Mae Kong, and since the Mae Kong fetched up near Saigon this would hardly do, the timber being wanted in Bangkok, not in the capital of French Indo-China.   What else, then? the pioneers asked themselves.   How far, for instance, was the Mae Yome away?   A brief survey revealed that nowhere did the Mae Yome run within forty miles of the forest, nor were there any creeks big enough to help float the timber down part of the way. Should they construct a road, and cart the logs the whole forty miles—more in some places?   This was tried, but it was frightfully slow work; in the rains the road became a quagmire, and as all the work had to be done in the hot weather, the strain was too much

for the buffaloes, which died in scores. Dragging by
elephant would be even slower, nor could elephants
stand up to it, and the firm was considering abandoning the forest and cutting their losses, when Swan had
a brain-wave. Why not build a light railway?

Experts gaped, then scoffed. Look at the expense,
they said. A special staff, for instance, would have
to be engaged for the initial survey work, and how on
earth were all the rolling stock and lines and innumer-
able spare parts to be got out from England to their
destination? To Singapore, yes. To Bangkok, yes.
To Nakon, possibly. But what about the one hundred
and twenty miles of hilly jungle still remaining to be
covered? And even were the transport difficulties
surmounted, and the track laid, and the engines got
ready with full steam up, how were the latter to face
the steep gradients inevitable to such a surface?

Swan remained adamant. The job, he insisted,
could be done. He was summoned to England, and
stood before the directors. They told him the whole
show was ridiculous: that it would lose them a lot
of money: that even the firm approached for supplying the locos. admitted that the gradients involved
were impracticable: they informed Swan that he'd
ruin them all—then told him to go ahead with the
project!!

Swan built that railway, surveying every inch of it
himself, organising relays of bullock carts to bring
chunks of locos. from the railway head, training, with
the help of an engineer, forest coolies to become
firemen and drivers, setting the track—and finally
getting the logs skimming in a few hours over a
distance that would have taken buffaloes years. And

that, considering that Swan was an ordinary teak-wallah, with no technical qualifications whatever, was a triumph.

It was on this railway that I hopped in order to be taken down to Swan's compound at Pohng, Pohng being the spot on the bank of the Mae Yome where the logs were taken off the trucks and rolled down into the river. As we flashed along, up and down gradients that made my hair stand on end and reminded me of the scenic railway in the Exhibition, I saw an occasional jungle shanty go by, and noticed that they were built on absurdly tall stilts. Whoever had made them, I reflected, had had an unusual desire to get off the ground, and it wasn't until I had seen several more such shanties, all a good twenty feet above the earth, that I realised we were passing through the territory once covered by the famous man-eater of Muang Pohng.

This man-eater, like the man-eaters of Tsavo in Colonel Patterson's well-known book, practically put an end to the working of the railway very soon after it started; and the brute would have gone *on* stopping operations had it not had to deal with Swan, the man whom nothing and no one could kill. If another teak-wallah had been in Swan's place, he would speedily have provided yet another meal for the killer—but here's to the story itself, as related to me by Swan in his Pohng bungalow when I arrived there.

The trouble began, said Swan, through a native, who was stealing a ride on a log on one of the trucks, overbalancing, falling off, and being decapitated by the wheels of the following truck. The train was stopped, but the man was beyond all human aid, and as it is a rule of the country that when a man is killed accidentally his body must be left where it is for inspection by the nearest headman (the equivalent of our " don't-touch-anything-till-the-police-arrive " practice), the train continued on down to Pohng, where Swan made an immediate report to the *poo yai ban*. By this time it was nearly dark, so it was impossible to visit the body that night, and when Swan, accompanied by the headman, set out early next morning, they found to their horror that only the head remained by the rails, the body having been dragged into some bushes and partly devoured. From the tracks it was obvious that a tiger, or rather a tigress as she turned out to be, had come accidentally upon the corpse and made a meal of it.

" That," went on Swan to me, " gave her her taste for human flesh. A couple of days later one of the coolies working on the line was taken, and then, as if that wasn't enough, she entered one of the coolies' huts, where about a dozen were sleeping in a row, and seized, not the outside man, but one sleeping well inside. She had to step over several to get at him, and the others were awakened by the brute dragging him over them. Grim, wasn't it? Well, that started the terror."

Swan went on to relate to me how man after man was taken, all traffic on the railway ceased, as the coolies—small blame to them—could not be induced to work on the lonely, jungle-fringed track, and everywhere throughout the district fear lay over the land like a pall. The merest rustle of a leaf, the shiver of a pool, the scamper of a rat, became sounds portending doom. MAN-EATER! Only one who has lived in the jungle can realise the truly appalling significance of the term.

Gendarmes were sent out from the nearest big native town, only to return after days of fruitless endeavour. Fearless forest hunters stalked the she-fiend, traps were laid, pits dug, and poison was smeared on baits. All, however, in vain, for the tigress had the cunning of the devil.

The list of killings mounted and mounted. Finally, no less than twenty-nine of the firm's employees or their friends and relations were slain, this apart from the very considerable number of victims the tigress must have claimed from the scattered jungle villages.

"Of course I sat up for her frequently," Swan informed me. "Remember Thorpe? Well, he came out to give me a hand, and we sat up together one night over the remains of a native. I suppose the eeriness of the show had affected Thorpe, for suddenly he was taken darned queer, and I was afraid of him falling off the *machan*, which was only a small, roughly built affair. Needless to say, the tigress didn't come *that* night."

It is strange how often comedy and tragedy go hand-in-hand. I pictured the scene not so far from the comfortable bungalow in which I now sat with Swan; the pathetic, mangled remains of the native beneath the tree: the ghoul perhaps slinking to and fro in the surrounding jungle, her crafty brain working as to whether to make a fresh kill or to return to the old: poor Thorpe, shivering and shaking with sickness and ague, perched on the tiny, hastily constructed platform, with Swan frantically clutching on to him. And over all the brooding stillness of the tropical forest. Truly a macaberesque situation.

" The end happened this way," went on Swan. " I was in camp one afternoon when news came of a villager having been killed about a mile away. Took a couple of Kamoo coolies with me, one of 'em having a gun, and when we'd found the corpse I sent the men up a tree near by, and then started walking back to my bungalow for my rifle."

This was typical of Swan. He was walking, unarmed and alone, in the immediate vicinity of the tigress and just at the time she was likely to return to her kill. Any other man would, of course, have been devoured for a certainty.

" Hadn't made more than a hundred yards or so, when I heard a bang behind me which told me that the Kamoo with the gun had let it off. So I walked back to see what had happened."

*He walked back to see what had happened.* To find, in all probability, a wounded and infuriated tigress by the tree!

What he did discover was the man-eater stone dead beside its victim, slain by a trembling Kamoo coolie who normally couldn't have hit the proverbial haystack.

Thus ended the terror. The tigress, incidentally, turned out to be a magnificent animal, in the prime of condition and with a perfect skin.

.    .    .    .    .

The arrangements for my return journey were as follows. For the neap of the Upper Mae Yome from Pohng I was to have one small dug-out for myself, but as this portion of the river was nothing but a succession of rapids, the use of the usual large boat for my kit was out of the question and I would have to rely on carrier coolies. The banks of the Mae Yome were apparently too rough to permit the men following down them, so, on Swan's advice, each day they were to cut inland a little, then turn and follow folds in the ground going parallel to the river as far as I reckoned I would get down by boat, after which they were to cut back to the river and rejoin me. It all sounded rather problematical, but there was no other method of accomplishing the neap.

Arrived at Keng Sua Ten, the rapids just above the mouth of the Mae Ngow—an eight-day neap—I was to mark the southernmost log I had counted for Orwell's information, then climb up the main Mae Yome watershed and drop down into the Mae Tang. Here I would be in familiar territory and only a few miles from Muang Ngow. At Muang Ngow I was to pay off the carrier coolies, then continue on to Nakon by pony and bullock-cart. A two-day train journey to Bangkok, a three-day trip in the *Kuala* down the Gulf of Siam, and I would then board the Dutch vessel that was taking me back to England. Altogether, a pretty varied journey was in front of me, and rather more so than I guessed.

I said good-bye to Swan, who waved to me from the bank, my carrier coolies and servants moved off on foot and disappeared from sight, and I started off down-stream in the little dug-out, my sole companions being two Lao paddlers. As it would be cooler marching through jungle than sitting in the dug-out, I had directed Sclave to follow my servants.

The country the river went through was very wild; steep jungle-clad banks loomed above us, rapids

ELEPHANTS DRAGGING DOWN DRY SIDE CREEK.

were even more numerous than I had expected, and of native villages there wasn't a sign. At four-thirty in the afternoon I saw my tent looming up ahead on a tiny bar of gravel, and knew that my coolies, who had conferred with my boatmen before starting off, had timed things to a nicety.

Next day, the Siamese jungle, as if deeming me worthy of the honour, opened its heart to me by showing me a tiger. I had just had tiffin under the shade of a tree, and to stretch my legs was wandering a little way down the bank, leaving my paddlers finishing their rice in the dug-out. I had made about a hundred yards when a slight movement on the opposite bank attracted my attention. Sensing instinctively that it must be some wild animal, I froze to immobility and turned my head cautiously, to see a great tiger emerging from the forest. At the point where he appeared, the bank sloped gradually to the river's edge, and, bathed in brilliant sunshine, he strolled leisurely to the water and began drinking in exactly the same position as a domestic cat—crouching down with shoulders humped.

Luckily my bank was in shadow, and since my khaki jungle-kit blended fairly well with the green of the background, I reckoned that he wouldn't notice me, provided he kept to his side of the river and didn't try to cross over. As for his smelling me, I knew that a tiger's scent is poor, and in any case what little wind there was, was blowing from him to me. I must, though, I knew, keep perfectly still.

As I watched, with my heart pounding more from excitement than from fear, great ripples ran out from his savage head, and I remember wondering whether

R

he minded getting his whiskers wet. The muscles on his shoulders mounded up in great lumps as he stooped, giving an impression of tremendous latent strength; *now* I could understand how tigers had been known to clear a fence with a small bullock in their jaws, and how they could eat as much as sixty pounds of meat at a sitting.

Presently he rose, turned sideways to me, and stretched out one leg behind him. In the brilliant sunshine every line of him was fully revealed to me; the stripes were much darker than I would have expected, and he looked much more *solid* than a Zoo animal. Heavy of shoulder, lean of flank, the small ears cocked, the great ringed face fiercely calm with the knowledge of absolute sovereignty, he stood thus for a few moments, then he wheeled and loped, softly yet with an impression of great weight, up the bank and the jungle swallowed him.

It was then fear seized me and I ran back to the dug-out, shouting " *seea*." The scared faces of my paddlers looked up at me. " *Seea*," I shouted again, " *pai pun leu*."

" *Seea?* " Already my men were frantically pushing off, their dusky countenances betraying the most comical mixture of excitement and terror. I jumped in, and the boat made really remarkable going down the next few bends, any odd logs encountered getting only the very briefest scrutiny, I fear.

The incident left me with a lingering sense of acute satisfaction; in gazing upon that wonderful wild thing, it had been given to me to see sheer beauty.

Two afternoons later, when about half-way down to Keng Sua Ten, I had a most unpleasant experience.

Four-thirty came and went with no sign of my camp showing up ahead, and when five o'clock arrived I feared that we might have overshot the mark and that the coolies had debouched on to the river at some point *behind* us.

" Where," I asked my paddlers, " did you arrange to meet the camp this evening? "

" At the mouth of the *Hwe* Bong," they replied.

Numerous little *hwes*, I should explain, or side-streams, ran into the Mae Yome, each of which, in spite of the loneliness of the country, seemed to possess a name known to all passers-by.

" And where is the *Hwe* Bong? " I demanded. " Are you sure we haven't passed it? "

They were quite sure, and we pushed on as fast as we could go. As it grew later and later it became increasingly evident that for the coolies to have got as far as this they would have had to travel tremend-ously fast, especially as very little timber had been encountered since the morning, with the result that we in the dug-out had made good progress all day. Finally, as if to add to our discomfiture, the dug-out jammed between two rocks while we were shooting a rapid. I got out to help the paddlers, and the three of us, standing waist-deep in the bubbling, mounding water, tugged and heaved at the craft.

In vain. We could not budge it an inch, and since the light was failing there was no alternative but to leave it wedged where it was and push on—or back?—on foot. Against my usual habit, my gun and cash-box were with my coolies under the special charge of the boy, as owing to the numerous rapids I had feared they might be lost if the dug-out capsized; their absence proved most fortunate now, for their weights would have proved sad handicaps in our present predicament, and all I had with me were the clothes I stood up in, an empty tin carrier that had held my cold tiffin, and a jar of filtered water. Leaving the latter two articles behind in the dug-out, we waded to the bank.

Again, where was this elusive *Hwe* Bong? One paddler confessed that after all we might have passed it, but the other was still certain we had not, and since to climb back uphill along the rough bank was impossible in the failing light, there was nothing but to go on down the bank. After shouting several times in the hopes of hearing an answering hail from somewhere, and receiving only the mocking echoes of our own voices, we started off.

I was wearing gym shoes—I never had boots on while neaping—shirt and shorts, and scrambling along the uneven, rough, jungle-clad bank proved a nightmare. I slipped and slithered and stumbled and fell, scratching my legs freely, and after an hour of this sort of thing it became too dark to proceed any further. A faint glimmer showing up against the dead black of the jungle on our left (the river being on our right), one of the paddlers said it might prove to be a clearing, or even a deserted *hai* with a *pang* in the middle in which we might sleep. Squatting down on the ground, I sent them to investigate.

As I sat there alone in the dark I was neither frightened nor depressed. I simply mused, I recollect quite clearly, on the extraordinary kinds of situations a man finds himself in at times. I also summoned one of my rather neglected phantom naval friends, and told him all about it. Tigers? They never even entered my head.

Presently the men returned, saying that indeed it was a deserted *hai* with a *pang*. I rose, but on getting to the edge of the *hai* found myself floundering helplessly about amongst the creepers and other snags that had sprung up over the place. My two Laos, who had eyes like cats, took my hands and guided me over, and soon the shape of the *pang* rose up ahead in the darkness. I then climbed up the rickety ladder, leaving the men, who would not enter though I asked them to, to make use of the space beneath. At first the little shanty, though not up to the standard of the " hotel " at Ban Min, seemed a godsend, but after a while I began to wish we had stayed out in the surrounding jungle. The bare, bamboo floor was infernally hard, for instance, and the place, which must have been deserted for several years, was most creepy. Every now and then a faint scuffle would sound in the ruined roof overhead, and once an unpleasant, crawling slither on the floor betokened the possibility of a snake being my sleeping companion. There also dawned on me the recollection that the Laos believed all deserted *pangs* to be haunted, and I knew for a fact that two of our Muang Ngow coolies had once spent, for a bet, the whole of a night in a haunted *pang* near the village, to be found dead next morning. They might have died of fright, of course, on hearing an owl or snake, *but*—I rose and made for the top of the ladder. Through the floor boards I could see the comforting flames of a tiny fire, and the night was turning chilly!

I joined the men below, and the three of us squatted

round the fire like three black crows. None of us had had anything to eat since the rather sketchy cold midday meal eaten in the dug-out, and we were certainly going to get no breakfast in the morning. For my part, I didn't feel in the least bit hungry, though I was longing for a cigarette, all mine having been finished long ago. Sleep being far away, I began working on plans for the morrow

The members of my camp would be wondering about where I was just as hard as I was wondering about them, and there was a danger, therefore, that we might go on chasing each other up and down the Mae Yome almost indefinitely. Clearly, then, *I* must do something definite. What? Obviously, I had better first walk back to the boat, which a little levering with some lengths of bamboo would soon set free, and then, if there were still no signs of any of my camp followers, start off *down-stream* as fast as my men could paddle. Without stopping for log counting, and with the current with us, we would make a tremendous distance, and the chances were that we would reach a village before nightfall. Here we would be assured of food and shelter, and from here we could send out searchers for the missing camp. Right! That was settled! And now for some sleep.

Sleep eluded me. One by one the paddlers rolled over by the fire, but I sat on, hands clasped round knees, occasionally shifting my position to feed the tiny fire with twigs. The silence was terrific; the ears sang with it. Outside my world of firelight the invisible jungle walled round the *hai*, guarding, as it were, us three weary mortals from the rest of mankind. In no way did that jungle seem hostile, and a marvellous peace stole over me; all worries, all fears dropped from my shoulders; strife had ceased to exist.

I suppose I did doze a little, but I was awake before dawn, and so were the boatmen from the cold. Directly it was light enough to move, we started up-stream the way we had come. A little more than an hour's toiling up the rough bank brought us to the place where we had left the boat, and here it was that real calamity stared us in the face. The boat had disappeared.

When we had recovered from the shock, we found that by sheer, brutal bad luck a rise of a foot or two had occurred in the river during the night, an almost unprecedented event in the hot season, and one caused probably by a thunderstorm far away to the north, and the dug-out had been carried away. It might have gone miles, or it might have turned over and be lying concealed amidst the thousands of rocks scattered along the river, but with it had gone *power*. All my plans were upset and we had now to rely upon our legs, which couldn't keep on the move for ever and which, compared to the dug-out, would get us along painfully slowly.

I decided to walk just a little distance further up-stream in case the camp was above us. The going became worse than ever, but each bend in the river lured us into thinking that round it the welcome sight of a tent and smoke would gladden our hearts, and we went on longer than I had intended. Finally, after a few last despairing shouts, we turned; there was now nothing but to keep on tramping down-stream till we came upon *something*.

After what seemed ages we repassed the place where

we had lost the boat, and noon found us back opposite the *hai* in which we had slept. *We had therefore walked the entire morning, from earliest daylight, absolutely for nothing.* The paddlers, as if the word *hai* signified " rest " for them, threw themselves flat on the bank, and though precious hours were slipping away, I followed their example.

I realised our position was really serious. We had had no food or proper rest for twenty-four hours, and how far away the nearest village might be I hadn't the ghost of a notion; the presence of the deserted *hai* would mean nothing, such places being found at times miles away from anywhere. The paddlers, who were supposed to know the river well, had become delightfully vague, and I resolved on one more shot at questioning them.

" How many bends from here is a village? " I asked them. " You are boatmen. You are boatmen specially hired because you know the river. Tell me."

" *Bor hoo, nai.*"

" *Bor hoo, nai.*"

They didn't know! Surely they must have *some* idea! Then it occurred to me that they were doing the brown man's reputed trick of lying down and dying. They were tired. They were empty. They were lost. Of what use was any more effort? Since they had to pass out anyhow, it was better to do so peacefully and gently. Simultaneously it occurred to me that I must give a display of the sturdy valour usually associated with the men of my race, so I rose to my feet and I said, in my loudest and most formidable manner:

" Get up! "

They got up, slowly and reluctantly, admittedly, but—they got up. I placed myself in between them, on the grounds that if necessary I could kick one forward while pulling the other, and after turning them so that they faced down-stream, I said:

" We will walk."

We began to walk. We went on walking. We walked and walked and walked, outrivalling Felix, the only times we stopped being when we slipped and fell. On and on and on, up and down the slopes of that appalling bank we went, I keeping as far as was possible a watch on the river below for the missing boat.

Two o'clock came and went, three o'clock, four o'clock, and still we slogged ahead. I can hear the pad, pad, slip, slither, pad, pad, pad of my gym-shoed feet yet. Fortunately the men were giving me no trouble, having relapsed into a sort of trance, while I felt as if I could go on walking for ever. Even food didn't make the slightest appeal to me. I suppose I had passed beyond any particular emotion.

When five o'clock had gone, and the glaring sun was beginning to sink below the fringe of trees, I realised that, if we didn't come upon either the camp or a village in another hour, and consequently had to spend yet another night in the jungle, our chances of survival would be small. I was in a low state of health to begin with, and though I still didn't feel in the least bit tired, sooner or later the collapse must come, and when it did it would be all the more complete for having held off for so long. As for the two Laos who accompanied me, I was sure they would crack up at any moment.

Could we live for a while on what we could snatch from river and jungle till somebody found us? Decidedly no! Even were my companions resourceful, which at the moment they certainly were not, we had no means of catching fish or animals, and of berries and the like I had seen nothing.

Pad, pad, pad. Nearly six o'clock. Pad, pad, pad. I was beginning to despair, when—lo!—a high, whining chant, exactly the kind of chant I had heard when nearly benighted near Nakon on the neap of the Upper Mae Wang, sounded in the distance ahead of us. We stopped and listened with almost painful intensity. Yes, there it was again: two natives, singing their way homewards.

The lethargy left my companions, and we all three started scrambling as fast as we could down along the bank, shouting hoarsely. After a hectic few minutes we came upon two brown, loin-clothed gentlemen who regarded us with a stare of mild interest and slight distaste.

" A village," we panted to them. " A village."

" A village," they replied casually, quite offensively casually, " yes, there is one down there. We know. We happen to live in it." (This in spite of the fact that surely it must be the most important village in the entire world.)

We followed them to it, and very soon I was squatting in the headman's hut, awaiting with shudders the arrival of the inevitable ducks' eggs and rice, for still I didn't feel hungry; indeed, oysters or caviare would have nauseated me.

I hadn't been there half an hour when my camp turned up. Where they had been I was never able to discover, in spite of a lot of explanations on the part of my servants and coolies. But it was lovely to smoke a cigarette and to have little Sclave, who I don't think had spent a night away from me for very many months, slobbering with joy to be with me again.

I clearly remember that cigarette. And I clearly remember how suddenly I threw it away unfinished; in a little over a week from now I would have left my dog for good.

## CHAPTER EIGHTEEN

## FAREWELL TO THE TEAK FOREST

CURIOUSLY enough, I felt no after-effects whatever from those trying thirty hours. I let all hands have a rest next day, and sent some villagers out for the lost dug-out, which they found stranded below the village. The day after, I neaped back over the stretch I had missed, then resumed the journey proper.

In due course I reached Keng Sua Ten, the big rapids in the Mae Yome a few bends above the mouth of the Mae Ngow. Here I paid off the boatmen, then with my carrier coolies and servants climbed up the great main river watershed in order to drop over into the familiar Mae Tang.

At the top I paused in order to gaze upon the Mae Yome far below me. I saw slopes of bamboo brakes, and trees without number, and patches of bare, sun-browned earth out of which the sweet-scented grass would rise at the break of the rains. A faint breeze, pure as only a breeze can be that has travelled over miles and miles of country untainted by civilisation, caressed my cheeks and moaned in the vent-hole of my helmet. Green parrakeets flashed, and suddenly a giant hornbill passed with his raucous " kok-kok-kok." In the distant blue a kite hovered. The Mae Yome itself seemed wrapped in silence, save where a dull murmur rose from the Keng.

I took the steep descent of the sources of the Mae

Tang, every step bringing me further into the Mae Ngow basin. In a patch of cool evergreen I passed through one of our elephant rest-camps; tuskers were browsing and grazing on either side of the little track we followed, their forms like black balloons amongst the trees, their tusks like wands, the sounds of their feeding like the snapping and crackling of fire.

The steepness of the descent lessened, and the Mae Tang, from a succession of waterfalls, turned to a normal river-bed sloping gradually down to its parent Mae Ngow. The bed was dry, with only an occasional pool showing, and at one o'clock in the afternoon, when the heat was singing in the tall trees, I gave orders to camp by one of the pools. We were yet twelve miles from the compound at Muang Ngow, a distance we would cover on the morrow.

I think that evening was the saddest one I have ever spent. This was the last time I would sleep in a tent in the Muang Ngow forest, or any other tropical forest; and I felt like a second Mowgli, leaving his jungle surroundings to return to the haunts of man. I forgot the hell of the rains, the fevers, the discomforts; I remembered the wonders of a cold weather morning, with the mists rising like smoke from the rivers and the dewdrops sparkling as the sun came forth; I remembered the utter serenity that descends upon one with the lengthening of the jungle shadows, a serenity so beautiful that no pen can possibly describe it. It was as though through the sufferings of Hell I had attained to Heaven, only to lose that Heaven now it was mine.

The light faded over the burnt-out forest, the opposite bank showing black and straight against the

increasing darkness of the sky. The backs of my
coolies bending over their evening rice made brooding
contours. The fires flickered and the shrill of the
cicalas ceased. I walked into my tent. Inside it
little Sclave, all innocent of the parting before him,
smiled at me with ears and eyes.

.　　　.　　　.　　　.　　　.　　　.

I was up early, and we struck camp. Soon we
gained the cart-road down which I had ridden on that
stormy evening when the missionary doctor had
passed through, and before long the Muang Ngow
paddy-fields, their stubble glaring in the sun, stretched
before us. Across them we marched, a long line of
slowly moving humanity, and reached the red-mouthed
*nagas* guarding the wall surrounding the little temple.
Within, shaven-headed, yellow-robed novices moved
quietly, and, leaving them behind us, we came to the
village street. On then, through the tiny market-
place, where brown men, women and children
salaamed shyly to one of the white lords of the Great
Company, and I was in the compound, where I put
up in the junior assistants' bungalow.

That afternoon a great black cloud rode up over the
tree-clad horizon. I thought a thunderstorm was
coming, but instead a terrific hailstorm broke. I
have never seen such hail anywhere, save once in
Folkestone; the whole of the huge compound became
a swirling white mass in which shapes could be dis-
tinguished but dimly, and the temperature dropped
with unheard-of rapidity: from 100° to 60° in under
an hour.

Through the storm Orwell came riding in on the
grey mare that looked part of the storm itself. He

had been out on a jungle trip and, hearing that I had arrived, ridden in to say good-bye. He decided to stay the night owing to the weather, and dined with me. We talked of different matters, but all the time there was something unsaid between us; Muang Ngow was part of his life, and he knew what I must be feeling.

On the morrow we approached our ponies, he to take the low road for the jungle, I the high road for Nakon. We shook hands, then with a brief " so long," he mounted and galloped off into the green.

I left the compound, with its smooth lawns and beds of roses and bungalows and little cool office, and rode slowly through the village street, the inhabitants now salaaming good-bye to the white master they had heard was returning to the Outside Country. Instead of branching left to go up to the Mae Tang as I had so often done before, I went straight on down a dip in the road till, passing the last of the shanties, I arrived at the ford crossing the thinly running Mae Ngow. As ever, I jerked at the reins of my pony to prevent him from drinking at the start of a journey, then, after splashing through the water, we gained the road that, skirting more paddy-fields, rose to breast the distant pass leading out of the Mae Ngow watershed.

With Sclave at my pony's heels, and the bullock-carts containing my kit squeaking and groaning behind him, I moved forward leisurely, drinking in every detail of the landscape. We camped at Hwe Tark, where the company owned a little bungalow built on a knoll overlooking the *hwe*, or stream. The bungalow was surrounded by a little hilly compound wherein teak trees grew, and the place was a favourite

spot of mine. As the light failed, I leant over the
verandah and stared at a jungle fire that flickered on
the heights opposite. Presently a little Lao family
came down the almost dry bed of the stream and made
preparations for staying the night immediately below
the compound. They put down their bundles, cut a
few lengths of bamboo and some big leaves from the
fringing jungle, and pulled some grass out of the dry
water-course. The grass for their beds, the leaves
and bamboo for their house, they quickly settled
down—father, mother, small daughter and one sloe-
eyed babe. Fires were lit, the rice was cooked, and
darkness found the family secure and happy. The
simple beauty of this little scene lingers with me yet.

Next day I crossed the Mae Lah valley, *my* old
familiar valley where I had first been put on to
girdling inspection, then I climbed up the long pass
leading out of the Mae Ngow forest. I turned in the
saddle for an instant to look down upon the vast,
rolling sea of trees, and then I was riding along the
rock-fringed road leading to Ta Nyong. The night
before reaching Nakon found me in the temple at
Sadet, with the same old ornaments tinkling in the
roof and the same bronze Buddha staring eternally
before him. And I thought of how, five years gone
by, here had been my first night of jungle adventure.
And I thought of all that had gone between.

In Nakon I sold my ponies, my saddlery, my gun
and pistol, and various other kit that would be useless
in England, and the morning arrived when I was to
catch the south-bound train for Bangkok. I could
not take little Sclave home with me, for there was not
only the six months' quarantine to be considered, but

he was getting old and I doubted whether he would survive the cold. I was therefore giving him to my boy, who was very fond of him, but I knew he would miss me terribly, especially as during this last year we had grown more attached to one another if possible than ever. (I heard later that he died soon after I left.)

The gharry rolled up to the bungalow to take me to the railway station. Out of the corner of my eye I saw Sclave's little black-and-white figure on the verandah. He had detected nothing wrong in the recent bustle and packing, for that was part of a teak-wallah's job, and so far as the gharry was concerned, we often hired them while in Nakon. I walked straight past little Sclave without so much as looking at him or giving him a farewell pat, and got in the gharry. The F.M., and others, would be down at the station to see me off, and I did not wish to make an exhibition of myself. I have never had a dog again, and I never will.

I said good-bye to the F.M., boarded the train, and soon we were running between the tree-clad hills. I had one more glimpse of the Mae Yome as we crossed the bridge, then the flat, uninteresting plains of Central Siam were reached, and for me the jungle was gone for ever.

# INDEX

# INDEX

**Some other Oxford Paperbacks for readers interested in Central Asia, China and South-East Asia, past and present**

## CAMBODIA

GEORGE COEDÈS
Angkor: An Introduction

## CENTRAL ASIA

PETER FLEMING
Bayonets to Lhasa

LADY MACARTNEY
An English Lady in Chinese
Turkestan

ALBERT VON LE COQ
Buried Treasures of Chinese
Turkestan

AITCHEN WU
Turkistan Tumult

## CHINA

HAROLD ACTON
Peonies and Ponies

ERNEST BRAMAH
Kai Lung's Golden Hours

ANN BRIDGE
The Ginger Griffin

PETER FLEMING
The Siege at Peking

CORRINNE LAMB
The Chinese Festive Board

W. SOMERSET MAUGHAM
On a Chinese Screen*

G. E. MORRISON
An Australian in China

OSBERT SITWELL
Escape with Me! An Oriental
Sketch-book

## INDONESIA

S. TAKDIR ALISJAHBANA
Indonesia: Social and Cultural
Revolution

DAVID ATTENBOROUGH
Zoo Quest for a Dragon*

VICKI BAUM
A Tale from Bali*

MIGUEL COVARRUBIAS
Island of Bali*

BERYL DE ZOETE AND
WALTER SPIES
Dance and Drama in Bali

AUGUSTA DE WIT
Java: Facts and Fancies

JACQUES DUMARCAY
Borobudur

JACQUES DUMARCAY
The Temples of Java

JENNIFER LINDSAY
Javanese Gamelan

EDWIN M. LOEB
Sumatra: Its History and People

MOCHTAR LUBIS
Twilight in Djakarta

MADELON H. LULOFS
Coolie*

ANNA MATHEWS
The Night of Purnama

COLIN McPHEE
A House in Bali*

HICKMAN POWELL
The Last Paradise

E. R. SCIDMORE
Java, Garden of the East

MICHAEL SMITHIES
Yogyakarta

LADISLAO SZÉKELY
Tropic Fever: The Adventures of
a Planter in Sumatra

EDWARD C. VAN NESS AND
SHITA PRAWIROHARDJO
Javanese Wayang Kulit

## MALAYSIA

ABDULLAH ABDUL KADIR
The Hikayat Abdullah

ISABELLA L. BIRD
The Golden Chersonese: Travels
in Malaya in 1879

PIERRE BOULLE
Sacrilege in Malaya

MARGARET BROOKE
RANEE OF SARAWAK
My Life in Sarawak

C. C. BROWN (Editor)
Sejarah Melayu or Malay Annals

COLIN N. CRISSWELL
Rajah Charles Brooke: Monarch
of All He Surveyed

K. M. ENDICOTT
An Analysis of Malay Magic

HENRI FAUCONNIER
The Soul of Malaya

W. R. GEDDES
Nine Dayak Nights

JOHN D. GIMLETTE
Malay Poisons and Charm Cures

JOHN D. GIMLETTE AND
H. W. THOMSON
A Dictionary of Malayan
Medicine

A. G. GLENISTER
The Birds of the Malay Peninsula,
Singapore and Penang

C.W. HARRISON
Illustrated Guide to the Federated
Malay States (1923)

TOM HARRISSON
World Within: A Borneo Story

DENNIS HOLMAN
Noone of the Ulu

CHARLES HOSE
The Field-Book of a Jungle-Wallah

SYBIL KATHIGASU
No Dram of Mercy

MALCOLM MacDONALD
Borneo People*

SOMERSET MAUGHAM
The Casuarina Tree*

AMBROSE B. RATHBORNE
Camping and Tramping in Malaya

ROBERT W. C. SHELFORD
A Naturalist in Borneo

J. T. THOMSON
Glimpses into Life in Malayan Lands

RICHARD WINSTEDT
The Malay Magician

## PHILIPPINES

AUSTIN COATES
Rizal

## SINGAPORE

PATRICK ANDERSON
Snake Wine: A Singapore Episode

ROLAND BRADDELL
The Lights of Singapore

R. W. E. HARPER AND
HARRY MILLER
Singapore Mutiny

JANET LIM
Sold for Silver

G. M. REITH
Handbook to Singapore (1907)

J. D. VAUGHAN
The Manners and Customs of the
Chinese of the Straits Settlements

C. E. WURTZBURG
Raffles of the Eastern Isles

## THAILAND

CARL BOCK
Temples and Elephants

REGINALD CAMPBELL
Teak-Wallah

MALCOLM SMITH
A Physician at the Court of Siam

ERNEST YOUNG
The Kingdom of the Yellow Robe

*Titles marked with an asterisk have restricted rights*